PENGUIN B

THE SILENCE BEYOND

SELECTED WORKS BY MICHAEL KING

At the Edge of Memory: A Family Story

Being Pakeha Now: Reflections and Recollections of a White Native

The Death of the Rainbow Warrior

Frank Sargeson: A Life

God's Farthest Outpost: A History of Catholics in New New Zealand

An Inward Sun: The World of Janet Frame

A Land Apart: The Chatham Islands of New Zealand (with Robin Morrison)

Maori: A Photographic and Social History

Moko: Maori Tattooing in the 20th Century (with Marti Friedlander)

Moriori: A People Rediscovered

New Zealanders at War

Nga Iwi o te Motu: One Thousand Years of Maori History

The Penguin History of New Zealand

Te Ao Hurihuri: Aspects of Maoritanga

Te Puea: A Life

Tread Softly For You Tread on My Life

Whina: A Biography of Whina Cooper

Wrestling with the Angel: A Life of Janet Frame

THE SILENCE BEYOND

SELECTED WRITINGS BY MICHAEL KING

With an introduction
by Rachael King

PENGUIN BOOKS

PENGUIN BOOKS
Published by the Penguin Group
Penguin Group (NZ), 67 Apollo Drive, Rosedale,
Auckland 0632, New Zealand (a division of Pearson New Zealand Ltd)
Penguin Group (USA) Inc., 375 Hudson Street,
New York, New York 10014, USA
Penguin Group (Canada), 90 Eglinton Avenue East, Suite 700, Toronto,
Ontario, M4P 2Y3, Canada (a division of Pearson Penguin Canada Inc.)
Penguin Books Ltd, 80 Strand, London, WC2R 0RL, England
Penguin Ireland, 25 St Stephen's Green,
Dublin 2, Ireland (a division of Penguin Books Ltd)
Penguin Group (Australia), 250 Camberwell Road, Camberwell,
Victoria 3124, Australia (a division of Pearson Australia Group Pty Ltd)
Penguin Books India Pvt Ltd, 11, Community Centre,
Panchsheel Park, New Delhi – 110 017, India
Penguin Books (South Africa) (Pty) Ltd, 24 Sturdee Avenue,
Rosebank, Johannesburg 2196, South Africa

Penguin Books Ltd, Registered Offices: 80 Strand, London, WC2R 0RL, England

First published by Penguin Group (NZ), 2011
1 3 5 7 9 10 8 6 4 2

Designed and typeset by Anna Egan-Reid © Penguin Group (NZ)
Printed in Australia by McPherson's Printing Group

ISBN 9780143565567

A catalogue record for this book is available
from the National Library of New Zealand.

www.penguin.co.nz

Contents

Introduction

One day in the late 1990s, when my father was working on his biography of Janet Frame, I was driving with him through Auckland city. Waiting at a set of traffic lights, I asked how the book was going, and he confirmed it was going very well. 'And who would you like to write your biography?' I was making conversation but was genuinely interested in who he thought might be up to the job.

'Nobody!' was his indignant reply. 'I don't want somebody poking about in my private business!'

The irony of the biographer as reluctant subject was not lost on him, and while he chuckled after he said it, he never answered my question any other way.

Instead, I think he decided it was a job he would like to do himself.

At the time of his death in 2004, he had a contract with Penguin to write a memoir. And, as his own biographer, he kept his papers in an immaculately organised state, something akin, perhaps, to how he would have liked to find the papers of his previous subjects.

Dad willed all his papers to the Alexander Turnbull Library, but my brother Jonathan and I derived too much comfort and interest from sitting in his office, looking out over Wharekawa estuary at Opotutere and reading through them to let them go immediately.

Searching through a box by his desk one night, I came across several photocopies of an essay entitled 'The Silence Beyond'. It began: 'At the age of thirty I found out that my name was not my *real* name.' I knew the story, of course. That my grandfather's father had been Peter Crawley, that my great-grandmother, widowed by the Great War, changed her name and those of her children to King when she married a New Zealand soldier and moved from Glasgow. But as far as I knew, and for reasons which are clear in the essay, Dad had never told the story before, not in *Being Pakeha* or its later incarnation *Being Pakeha Now*, nor in any of his other work. In fact, a photograph in those books of Peter Crawley in his Scottish army uniform, complete with kilt, carries the caption 'my father's father'. And I knew that as long as my grandfather was alive, Dad would not have felt able to write fully about the circumstances that brought the family to New Zealand. So I knew, as I was reading it, that because my grandfather had survived his son by more than two years, I had in my hands a piece of writing that had never been published.

I wish I could have asked him what his intentions were for the piece. It may have been meant as the first chapter for a new book about his life and his family history, one unimpeded by his father's wish for privacy, or it could have been intended as a standalone piece, as it reads perfectly well as one.

One thing I knew was that it should be published, and together with my brother and with Geoff Walker at Penguin we came up with a plan to gather together a book of selected works, with 'The Silence Beyond' as a centrepiece.

The job was surprisingly easy. While we could no longer sift through boxes at our leisure but instead had to apply to read folders at the Turnbull Library, not only had Dad done a magnificent job of cataloguing his own work, in turn, the Turnbull staff had done a marvellous job of further cataloguing. Instead of having to trawl through everything, we simply had to order up folders labelled 'other published work' and 'speeches', which were spirited up from somewhere below. Discounting work that had appeared in 2001's *Tread Softly For You Tread On My Life*, we were still left with a significant amount of strong material: work that had appeared in anthologies, some long out of print, which people who had read his books may not have seen before; articles he had written for magazine and journals such as the *Listener* and *Landfall*; the odd snippet of work from his books; moving and personal tributes to friends who had passed on; and speeches he had given, such as the powerful and possibly controversial 'Maori and Pakeha: Which People and Culture Has Primacy?' at the 2003 Auckland Writers Festival.

While that talk showed his scalpel-sharp mind, we also wanted to showcase another side to him, a side that his friends and colleagues knew well, but that perhaps wasn't so widely known to the public at large – Michael King the comedian. His wit was cheeky, subversive even, and his love of gossip shocking (only recently has his role as *Quote Unquote*'s gossip columnist Courtenay Plaice, and his regular contributions to *Metro*'s Felicity Ferret page, been revealed to me).

In 'Remembering Dan and Winnie Davin', my father 'detected a tussle' in Dan 'between the obligations to declare what is true and reasonable and temptation to say what is clever or amusing', a tussle I suspect he often experienced himself. I remember once watching him introduce Anthony Beevor at an Auckland Writers Festival dinner, held at the same time as the Auckland Comedy Festival. Dad elicited as many laughs in that short opening as any stand-up comic I'd seen that week, and I told him so. He was a jovial presence at literary events and it is not just as a speaker and a writer that he is missed, but as the life of many parties, which he enjoyed in bursts away from his quiet, scholarly life at Opoutere. I hope some of these pieces convey that sense of fun.

Some of the work was painful to read. In 'Janet and the Birds', the speech he gave at Janet Frame's memorial service, he described the argument he and Janet had about whose death was portended by the daytime appearance of a morepork. The fact that they *both* died, so close together, makes it a skin-prickling piece to read, and when he describes the reception nationwide of the news of Frame's death, he could very well have been describing the effect on the country of his own death, right down to his appearance on the cover of the *Listener*.

In 'What I Believe', which outlines his personal faith, I found the words that later made their way into *Being Pakeha Now*: 'In the coming and going of the tides, in the rise of mist and the fall of rain, I see a reflection of the deepest mystery and pattern in all life: that of arrival and departure, of death and regeneration.' We chose these words to adorn Michael and his wife Maria's memorial headstone, which was made by Barry Brickell and erected in what is now the Michael King Memorial Reserve at Opoutere. With the headstone's position, next to a pohutukawa-shaded seat overlooking their beloved estuary, the words seemed apt.

Other words from 'What I Believe' seemed apposite as we went about selecting these pieces: 'I no longer believe that human life is eternal in the sense that we maintain our individual consciousness after death . . . however, I do believe in the power of literature and the arts to convey thought, feeling, even wisdom, from one generation to another. It is in this sense only that individuals achieve a degree of 'immortality'; and in the way in which they influence the lives of those with whom they come into contact, especially their descendants.'

He couldn't have known then the profound impact his legacy would have, not just on his descendants, but on the rest of New Zealand as well.

The 'silence beyond' invokes the ancestral silence Dad felt beyond his grandparents, which he set out to fill by exploring the lives of his antecedents. But of course, the phrase can be read in many ways, particularly as the title of a posthumous publication, and some readers may relate it to their own beliefs about what lies in store for us after we die. By leaving us these pieces to read, some for the first time, some again, my father is making sure that although he's gone, and no matter what he believed, his voice will be heard for some time to come.

Rachael King

1.

The Silence Beyond

At the age of thirty I found out that my name was not my *real* name. I also discovered antecedents on my father's side of the family of whom I had been entirely ignorant. This was an odd experience, and strangely disorienting for a person whose profession was historian and whose whole training had emphasised clarity, accuracy and precision. These disclosures forced me to re-think and to reconstruct my identity. They had been kept from me and my siblings because my father had experienced them as painful revelations in *his* adolescence and resolved to shut the door on the troubled past that his immediate family had left behind in the United Kingdom.

Growing up in New Zealand in the 1940s and 1950s I had believed that my family constituted a neat division of half-Irish and half-Scottish ancestry. The Irish side came via my mother's mother, Eleanor Tierney, whose father had migrated from County Mayo to the north of England in 1856 and married Isabel Laverty in Hexham-on-Tyne. It was through this Irish grandmother that we derived a sense of tradition, of belonging to a clan and a culture. Throughout my childhood I was swathed in the songs, stories and prayers of Irish Catholicism, and we kept in close touch with the remnants of my grandmother's family.

From my father's side, however, we knew little – so little, in fact, that every detail seemed the more precious for being sparse. There was my father and his sister and their mother, and an aunt, my grandmother's sister. They had all come from Scotland. There was an implicit script created to explain how they came to be in New Zealand. It went like this:

My father and my aunt had been born in Glasgow of Scottish-Presbyterian parentage. There were no other siblings. *Their* father, my Scottish grandfather, had been killed on the Western Front early in World War One. My Scottish grandmother had subsequently married a soldier who brought her small family to New Zealand and then died. From that time my grandmother raised her two children as a second-time widow. Later she remarried again, in 1936. We had no relatives in New Zealand by the name of King. They were all in Scotland and my grandmother had not remained in communication with them.

Such was the story that had evolved to conceal scars on the family psyche. It was plausible; it was unremarkable; and it was also, we would discover, almost wholly untrue. But it would take many years to discover what had actually happened to my father's family – which is also, of course, my own family.

The first crack in the screen erected by my father and grandmother was the mysterious information I gleaned when I was about five that we had cousins in the United States – cousins belonging to my father's side of the family. Their names were Raymond and Sharon and they had sent us Christmas presents (my older sister got a doll called Daphne and a fur muff). Precisely *how* we were related to them was not clear. I assumed that their surname was King. But none of the adults in the family would directly answer questions about them. It was not unusual for my father and his mother to be uncommunicative – this could be attributed to a supposedly dour Scottish disposition. (My grandmother's standard answer to questions about her age was to say that she was 'as old as my tongue and a little bit older than my teeth'.) What struck me as peculiar, however, was that my mother wouldn't discuss the matter, and she normally answered *all* my questions except the one about where babies came from.

The next pieces of perplexing evidence that came to light were photographs. My mother kept all the family pictures in a padded trunk, among her sewing and knitting implements. Some were in albums, some loose in boxes and envelopes. Usually she was the one who located them and brought them out to us. But on one occasion, when I was ten or eleven, I wanted to show a school friend some pictures of my father in 'the war' – for us there was only one, the Second World War – to prove that he had been there.

Going through the envelopes of loose pictures I came across three I hadn't seen before. One of a girl with curly blonde hair was marked 'Sharon'. One was of a good-looking boy in a long-trousered suit that children of his age would not wear in New Zealand: 'Raymond'. The third was of a blonde woman in a bathing suit, with one arm around a handsome man who looked strikingly like my father. It was inscribed, 'Pete and I on vacation in Atlantic City'.

When I asked my mother about the photographs, she looked flustered, so that I felt I had done something wrong by discovering them. But she showed no sign of being cross with me. The man, she said, was my father's older brother, Peter. He lived in Detroit and made cars. The woman was his wife, Pauline. 'Are they Raymond's and Sharon's mother and father?' 'Yes'. So, my father *did* have a brother in the United States and his name was Peter King. He made cars. He was good-looking. Perhaps he was famous? But, again, when I tried to discuss the matter with my father and grandmother, they were tight-lipped and projected an aura of palpable disapproval. Like sex, this was a subject simply not to be talked about.

I *did* talk about it with my brother and sisters, however. And we, familiar only with the face of American life presented in movies or in magazines such as *Saturday Evening Post* and *Good Housekeeping*, speculated about how our uncle and aunt might have lived, the certainty that they must be wealthy, the kind of house, limousine and home appliances they might have, and what our cousins might be like and whether they drank sodas and ate popcorn. This American family was more exotic and therefore more interesting to us than our known cousins in Newtown and Miramar, precisely because we knew so little about them and therefore had more room for them in our imaginations. We talked of visiting them when we were grown up, when *they* would be rich and famous, and it was as alluring a prospect as stepping into a Shirley Temple movie.

Throughout my childhood only one further document about my father's family came to light. I was visiting my grandmother and she promised to find a photograph of my father as a boy, to show me how much like him I was supposed to look. I insisted that she do so there and then, and – to my surprise, for she was not usually compliant – she did so. As she drew photographs from a chocolate box on the opposite side of the kitchen table, one fell out and lay facing me on the tablecloth. It showed a man in a tartan cap and a kilt standing beside a bicycle. I pounced on it. 'Who's that?' My grandmother took it off me and said, 'It's your grandfather.' 'What was his name?' 'Peter.' 'Peter King?' She hesitated, and then nodded. 'The same name as our uncle in America,' I said. My grandmother nodded and said nothing more, but looked displeased at the turn the conversation had taken.

For reasons I couldn't begin to understand, this was still a forbidden topic.

The years went by, and whenever people by the name of King asked me if we might be related, I gave the stock answer, and what I believed was an honest one: 'We have no relations in New Zealand by the name of King. They all live in Scotland and the United States.'

I learned nothing further about my father's family until I was thirty years old and about to travel to Europe and the United Kingdom for the first time. I wanted to apply for a certificate of patriality, which would give me certain advantages for entering, living and working in the United Kingdom – provided I could establish that one of my parents had been born there. That was a simple job, I thought. I wrote to my father and asked for a copy of his birth certificate.

I got no reply and so wrote again. This time he sent me copies of two documents: the birth certificate of one Lewis Crawley, born in Glasgow in 1914, son of Peter Crawley ('salesman of spiritous liquors') and Martha Crawley, *née* Lyon. Attached to this was a marriage certificate dated 1918 for Martha Crawley ('widow') and Arthur Robert King, whose address was given as Brougham Street, Wellington, and occupation as 'farmer'. The first thing that struck me was the surname Crawley, which I had never come across before outside the pages of William Makepeace Thackeray's *Vanity Fair*, where the family had been shabbily genteel aristocrats; the second shock was that anyone who lived in Brougham Street should call himself a farmer. There was not much opportunity for farming in Brougham Street, one of the oldest of Wellington's suburbs, even in 1918. My father's accompanying note said simply that I would have to present both documents, with my passport, to the British High Commission: one to show that he had been born Lewis Crawley in Glasgow; the other to explain how his name – and mine – came to be King.

I went to see him, but he had nothing further to tell me. Yes, his name had been Crawley. He had been brought up as King as a result of his mother's remarriage. He said he knew nothing about the Crawleys and didn't want to know anything. Nor did he know anything about the Kings. They were not, in any case, blood relations. There was no reason to discuss the matter. He had given me the information and documents I needed. The subject was closed.

It was not closed in *my* mind, which was now reverberating with surprise, and with further questions about what I viewed, after all, as my family too. I went straight to Miramar to see my grandmother. Gran, as we called her, was by this time eighty-six years old. Her third husband had died a decade earlier and she lived alone near the gasworks, tending her vegetable and flower gardens. Carnations grew spectacularly well in the sandy soil which made up the Miramar spit. She was still as I had always known her to be: tough, dour and Scottish. The only things that had changed in her old age were that she seemed to be shrinking from the effects of osteoporosis and her Glaswegian accent was, if anything, getting stronger.

On this particular morning she might have been feeling exceptionally well; or, perhaps, unguarded. I shall never know. But she talked about family matters – the *only* time she did this with me and, as far as I knew, with any member of the family since coming to New Zealand. In the course of this discussion she made what were, for me, astonishing revelations.

I had begun by explaining how I now knew about the Crawley connection and said that while I was in the United Kingdom I would visit Glasgow. I would like to see where she was born and to contact relatives, if she could tell me of any who might be still alive. She didn't say anything for a long time. She prepared the tea and laid out sandwiches and oatmeal biscuits in silence, and then put more wood in the kitchen stove. Then she leaned across the kitchen table. 'I'll tell you something the noo,' she said, 'but dinna go twittering to the others.' And she began to talk.

She said she had been born at 5 St Clair Street in Maryhill, Glasgow, in a two-roomed sandstone tenement apartment. She had had three sisters and three brothers, after one of whom, Lewis, her favourite, my father was named. Her mother died at home when she was five but had whispered to her, just before the end, to be sure to get hold of her birth certificate (that is, her mother's). When she was older and asked for it, her father refused to hand it over. Gran had not known that such documents were publicly available. This behaviour of her father's, coupled with the fact that expensive clothes arrived for her every Christmas from her mother's relations, the Toners, led her to believe that she was eligible for some kind of inheritance. When she was an adolescent, one of her mother's brothers sent an urgent message that she was to come and see him. But by the time she got the message he had died. What she wanted me to do, my grandmother said, was what she had wanted my *father* to do during the war: to track down whatever firm of solicitors had represented her mother's family and see if money was still being held for her (and this nearly sixty years after she had left Scotland).

She told me much more: about growing up in slum conditions, about being beaten by her unsympathetic father, about running away from home to work in a tobacconist's and then as a clippy on the Glasgow trams. Finally, for security – or so she believed – she married Peter Crawley, spirits salesman. They had had four children, one of whom had died in infancy.

Peter Crawley, the grandfather of whom I had known nothing until this day, was the oldest in a family of ten children. His father and his mother's parents had been born in Ireland. They were all Catholic, and Gran had had to have her own children baptised Catholic (including my 'Presybterian' father!) in order to marry Peter. Her mother-in-law

Mary Crawley was a large domineering woman who used to stand at the window of her tenement room on 12 July – the day of the Orangemen's Walk – and hurl abuse and the contents of her chamber pot on to the Protestants marching below. Peter had volunteered for the Gordon Highlanders on the outbreak of war and had been killed in September 1915 somewhere in France or Belgium (his body was never found). Mary Crawley then took charge of Peter junior, my father's older brother, because she felt sure that my grandmother would not continue to bring up the children Catholic (indeed, she did not). Later, she took him to Detroit in the United States.

My grandmother, in the meantime, met a part-Maori New Zealand soldier on leave in Glasgow: Artie King, a private in the First Otago Battalion. 'Part-Maori' was *his* description of himself. He told her that he had a farm in New Zealand and would take her and the children there if my grandmother married him. She, seduced more by the prospect of green fields and clean air than by the man courting her, eventually agreed. They married in Glasgow and sailed for New Zealand on the *Ionic* early in 1919.

The reality of life in New Zealand was a shock. She liked the country and the people well enough. The difficulties were with her husband, her husband's family, and their situation. The farm turned out to be a market garden in Mangere leased by King's Pakeha father and Maori mother. My grandmother was expected to work all day in the gardens for no more than food and keep, and to cook for the extended family at night. She and the children lived in one room attached to a ramshackle house and slept on sacks stretched over wooden frames. My grandmother did not like her new mother-in-law any more than she had liked her first one and they argued when they were together.

Artie King kept trying to get them away from Mangere by applying for one of the Rehab farms being made available for returned servicemen. But he was always turned down, apparently because he was Maori. Finally, my grandmother said, in frustration at having his hopes constantly dashed, he tried to explode a home-made bomb in the grounds of Parliament in Wellington and was arrested. (I doubted the likelihood of this story, but years later found the court report in a Wellington newspaper that confirmed it. Oddly, though, Arthur Robert King, labourer, was convicted only of 'behaving in a disorderly manner'. He was fined five pounds and default of payment was fixed at fourteen days' imprisonment. If he had indeed planned to blow up Parliament, then he had gotten off lightly.) My grandmother walked out on him at this point and brought up my aunt and my father on her own, in Wellington. Artie continued to turn up from time to time over the years, always asking for money. She did not know what became of him eventually.

I asked about her eldest son, Peter Crawley junior, in the United States. She said that she had heard nothing from or about him until my aunt saw a notice in the Miramar Post Office in the mid-1930s. It asked anyone knowing the whereabouts of Martha Crawley, who had migrated to New Zealand after the war, to communicate with Peter Crawley in Detroit. My aunt, whose name was also Martha, and who retained the surname Crawley until she married, did so. And for about a decade the New Zealand and American branches of the family had exchanged letters. Hence the photographs in our home of my cousins Raymond and Sharon. But contact was lost in about 1950, and my grandmother did not know what had become of the Detroit Crawleys. She said she had felt bad about giving up her first-born, but that Mary Crawley had convinced her that she, the child's grandmother, could give him a better life than Gran, a widowed, working solo mother.

I asked my grandmother finally why she had never spoken of these matters to us. She glared at me, as if the answer was self-evident. It was nobody else's business, she said, but her own; and what was passed was past. It was the present and the future that you had to look to. And it was with that unshakable attitude that she had survived.

I failed to find any relations in Glasgow, although one who *was* there at the time, I discovered later, was a Catholic priest named George Crawley, a first cousin of my father. I simply looked at the telephone directory, saw too many of the family names and gave up. Nor did I locate the fortune my grandmother was sure she had forsaken. But I did see some of the tenements in which she had lived, including 5 St Clair Street where she had been born, which was under demolition when I arrived. A week later and it would have been levelled. They were grim places where a film of dirt seemed to coat everything – streets, footpaths, shops and buildings. The gentrification of inner Glasgow, which would gain momentum in the following decade, had not yet begun. The dominant colours were black and grey, the populace in those places pasty and unhealthy looking. Unemployment was still widespread, many families still lived in only one or two rooms without amenities, and the major social features were truancy, vandalism and alcoholism. Even after the passage of nearly sixty years, the need my grandmother felt to emigrate was entirely comprehensible.

I made most spectacular progress in the Scottish Records Office in Edinburgh. There over two days, playing snakes and ladders with registrations of births, deaths and marriages, I moved my knowledge of that side of the family back several generations, to great-great-grandparents. It was a moving experience to read the names of people previously unknown to me from whom I descended – Crawleys, Cassidys, Lynches, Gleesons; and to see their marks, for many of them had been illiterate and authorised their rites of passage with crosses. It was moving too to see their occupations in industrial Glasgow, then the largest city in the Empire: slater, power loom beamer, India rubber worker, domestic servant; and some who had simply ended up in the workhouse.

I also managed, with the subsequent help of census records and a cousin, to trace the Crawleys back to County Armagh and County Down, where our great-great-grandfather John Crawley had been born in 1804. Further back than that it was impossible to go, for Ireland has no Catholic registrations beyond the nineteenth century. But John Crawley, somewhat to my disappointment, turned out to have joined the British Army (10th Foot Lincolnshire Regiment), had been posted to Portugal and the Ionian islands, and then, after twenty years, left the army at Tipperary and married Ellen Gleeson of that county. They returned to the north, to Newry, in the course of the Famine, and it was there that their three boys were born, including my father's grandfather Patrick Crawley. All three sons went to Glasgow in the early 1880s, evidently in search of employment.

The greatest surprise, however, came from my father's mother's side of the family. My 'Scottish' grandmother had not only married into an Irish-Catholic family, but her own mother too had Irish ancestry. That mother, one of my great-grandmothers, had been illegitimate. *Her* mother's family were Irish; her father's name was nowhere to be found. She had been brought up with Toner half-siblings, also Irish and Catholic, who came from County Armagh like the Crawleys. Was the missing inheritance my grandmother dreamed of the property of her unnamed maternal grandfather? Was it he who kept sending her presents each year via the Toner family? Suddenly what had at first seemed to me a foolish belief on my grandmother's part now had a plausible foundation. But how much of this did she know? I couldn't bring myself to tell her *any* of it, in case the details were new to her and became a source of further trauma; or in case she know of her mother's illegitimacy but was determined to keep it from the rest of the family. I *knew* it would all be new to my father, and hence said nothing at all to him about what I and subsequently my cousin were able to discover.

And there, so far as I was concerned, matters rested for another decade. My grandmother's temporary interest wilted when I told her that I had not been able to find an inheritance. My father showed no interest at all. And I had, for the time being, satisfied my own curiosity and filled in gaps in the family genealogy. I stored the new material away with other papers.

In 1985, however, a convergence of circumstances brought the family narrative back to the surface of my attention. I turned forty, which felt at the time like a rite of passage and fed introspection; my Scottish grandmother died just short of her ninety-fifth birthday; and I became chronically ill. Lying in bed, reflecting on life, death and kinship – themes I had already explored in the histories and biographies of other people – I began to draft a family memoir which I proposed to call *Being Pakeha*.

My original intention was to make something of the fact that Artie King, who had brought the family to New Zealand and given us his name, was Maori. This seemed ironic in the light of the then current debate over whether or not Pakeha people had any right to be in New Zealand; and in the light of my own preoccupation with Maori history, which had drawn criticism from some quarters because my lack of Maori ancestry. The relationship with Artie King and the circumstances in which he persuaded by grandmother to come to New Zealand was to be the starting point for a book that would allow me to end it on a cyclic note. I even had an arresting if not entirely accurate sentence: 'Of my four grandfathers, two were Irish, one English and one Maori' (in fact this would refer to two 'real' and two step-grandfathers).

And so, for the first time, I did some research on Artie King and his family. He had been born in Hokitika in 1889. His father had come from Dunedin. I could not trace the Maori connection, though my grandmother had said it was through Artie's mother. I began to wonder if she had been mistaken about this, until I located a photograph of King in army uniform. That seemed to dispose of any doubt: his features were unmistakably Polynesian.*

King's service record was passed on to me by the Ministry of Defence with some reluctance. Artie King had not been a model soldier. He had enlisted in the Otago Regiment early in 1915 and served at Gallipoli, and in France throughout the Western Front campaign. He is described as five foot six-and-a-half inches tall, weighing nine stone thirteen pounds, and having brown eyes, dark skin and black hair. He received a gunshot wound in the left leg at Armentières and wounds to the hand and chest at Citerne. The file records persistent offences including absence without leave and use of obscene language to officers. On one occasion he went 'missing in the field' for more than nine days – which sounds suspiciously like a desertion eventually reconsidered.

I also found, via his war pension documents, that he had died in 1963, after a career as an itinerant farm worker and a subsequent period of decline, in the Ranfurly Veterans' Home in Auckland. He had never remarried and he left no known descendants. I did manage to track down two of his nieces. One of them declined to let me into her house and informed that there was no property to inherit; the other was warmly helpful and gave me the photograph of King in uniform. She remembered him as a kind of 'wicked uncle', a ne'er do well, who would disappear for years at a time and then turn up unexpectedly at family functions. She had no information on the family's putative Maori connections.

I wove all this information together with the Crawley material into what was to be chapter one of *Being Pakeha*. Then I sent it to my father,

---

* Since doing this research a new possibility has occurred to me. The difficulty in linking the family with any known Maori family or tribal genealogy could spring from the fact that they were descended from one of the group of Chatham Island Moriori who settled in the south of the South Island in the 1850s. But, given that I have also written a history of Moriori, this may be drawing too long a bow of coincidence.

to gauge his response and to test its accuracy against his memory. I assumed, or rather hoped, that the death of his mother would make it easier for him to consider such matters and to discuss them with family. I was wrong. His response was immediate and unequivocal. He wrote:

> What you ask is impossible. I pulled the blind down on my past so long ago that it's sealed more thoroughly than Tut's tomb. I was furious about the unsettled background I came from and have gone out of my way to pretend that it didn't happen. The fact that I found out from an early age – from other children at school – that even my name wasn't my own, drove me deeper into a determination to wipe it all out. My mother and I avoided all discussion on these things. I never asked for information and she never offered any – and we were both happy to leave it at that. I don't want to go ratting round in the rubbish now.

The letter ended with a quotation:

> You're welcome to your family tree
> Its soil and roots are sour to me

The message was clear. If I published any information at that time in *Being Pakeha* about the King/Crawley dimension of family history my relationship with my father would be severely strained, possibly irreparably. So I did not. I erased the opening section as I had drafted it and the book lost the cyclic thematic shape that had originally underpinned it.

My curiosity was awakened again, however. The one potential source of family information that remained uninvestigated was my father's brother in the United States – the brother he did not even know he had until my aunt saw the request in the Miramar Post Office in 1934, when my father was twenty. All I knew was that his name was Peter

Crawley and that he had been living in Detroit up to about 1950. On impulse one afternoon I walked into the Mormon Library in Takapuna and asked if I could consult the Detroit telephone directory. There were two. By chance the first one I picked up was East Detroit and it had one listing for a P. Crawley. I wrote this number down, returned home and direct-dialled it.

A woman answered and the sound and tone of her voice suggested that I had woken her (I had: it was after 11 p.m. in Michigan). She asked what I wanted with what seemed to me to be understandable caution. I said I was trying to contact a Peter Crawley who had migrated to Detroit from Glasgow some time after 1919, and was that his number. There was a long pause. Then: 'Who wants to know?' I told her. There was an even longer pause. Then it all came out.

She said that her name was Pauline, and that was why the number was listed for P. Crawley. She was Peter Crawley's widow, my aunt by marriage. She and my uncle had been divorced and he had died in 1974, aged sixty-four. I asked about my cousins. Raymond too was dead. And Sharon, suffering long-term effects from a car accident, lived at home with her mother. We had a warm conversation and I filled her in with news of the New Zealand family.

The earlier contact with New Zealand had been initiated by Peter because he wanted to find out what had happened to his mother. Pauline had stopped writing to the family when she and Peter separated, however, because he hadn't wanted his mother, my grandmother, to know that this had occurred. She told me one further thing. Other members of the Crawley family had migrated from Glasgow to Detroit in the 1920s and one of them – an aunt of my father's – was still alive in her nineties.

After that discussion I remained in touch with Pauline Crawley by letter. Then, in 1988, I had an opportunity to travel to the United States and to meet my aunt, my cousin and other Crawley relatives for the first time. That visit to Detroit filled in most of the pieces missing from the family mosaic.

Great-aunt Alice Crawley, who – up to the year before I had arrived in Detroit – was still able to sing songs that the family carried to Scotland from County Armagh, was alive at the age of ninety-seven. But she had had a stroke that erased her memory and was now living in a rest home. Two of my father's older cousins in their eighties were there, however, and they remembered him and my aunt and grandmother well. As girls they had been roped in to wheel my father around Glasgow in his pram while my grandmother was at work. They seemed thrilled to meet me and to find out what had happened to the New Zealand branch of the family, of which they had heard nothing for almost fifty years. They were also able to provide me with much of the information I lacked, delivered in accents that were three-quarters Glaswegian and one-quarter American.

Cissy and Edith confirmed from oral tradition what I had already inferred from the documentary record: that the family – embracing all its Irish-Glaswegian branches – had left Ireland in the late nineteenth century to find employment in industrial Scotland. The migration to the United States in the 1920s had occurred for the same reason: to seek work and better living conditions. Unemployment was high in Glasgow at the time and several older members of the family had ended up in the workhouse; growing assembly lines in North America had the same appeal as factories had had at the time of Glasgow's florescence. And, as they had done when they left Ireland, the Crawleys migrated as an extended family.

It came about like this. My grandmother had left Glasgow for New Zealand with her Maori husband and two remaining children in 1919. Great-grandmother Crawley had used this fact to turn my father's brother against his mother. 'You see, she doesn't want you,' she told him. 'Otherwise she would never have gone to another country.' This notion hurt my uncle terribly and was probably a source of some of the problems he encountered as an adult.

Then, in 1923, Great-grandmother Crawley decided to move from Glasgow to Australia with her husband and my uncle, who was now aged thirteen. Did she have second thoughts about separating him from his mother? Did she think that by going to Australia Peter would be able to re-establish contact with his family across the Tasman Sea? We'll never know, because she was talked out of that plan.

A nephew, John Crawley, had previously moved to Minnesota, because his wife had sisters there. Work was not readily obtainable, however, and he shifted instead to Detroit, where the automobile industry was beginning to burgeon. Jobs – and jobs excessively well paid compared with those in Glasgow – were so plentiful that he sent word back to Scotland. In due course, throughout the 1920s, his brothers and sisters, aunt and uncle (my great-grandparents) and his Crawley cousins all joined him there.

My Crawley great-grandparents left Glasgow with my uncle Peter in 1923. By 1927 the elderly couple were dead. Patrick Crawley, employed as a night watchman, had succumbed to cirrhosis of the liver; and Great-grandmother Mary was killed by a hit-and-run driver. Peter, aged seventeen, was left to fend for himself. He fobbed off offers of assistance from the rest of the Crawleys. Instead, with a friend, he began jumping trains and travelled all over the United States in this way, picking up work where they could. They spent part of the Depression years prospecting on the worked-over goldfields in California.

Sometime in the early 1930s Peter returned to Detroit, the nearest place he had to a home in the United States, and began to work as a punch press operator for Zenith Carburettor. That's where my Aunt Pauline met him in 1934. She noticed him, and fell in love with him, because he was dapper and careful about his appearance in a messy job.

He wore a clean shirt to work every day and combed his hair whenever it became dishevelled. Three months after meeting they married. It was she who encouraged him to write to New Zealand in the hope of being able to contact his mother.

Domestic responsibilities, especially having children, persuaded my uncle to concentrate on work in a manner he had not done previously. He rose through factory ranks into management: to foreman at Zenith, and then to production manager and plant manager at Woodall Industries. A decade after their marriage, however, my aunt realised that he had a serious problem. He drank alcohol excessively. And when he drank he absented himself from work and home for days and sometimes weeks at a time. Pauline knew nothing about alcoholism, nor about how it could or should be treated. She just knew that the drinking was corrosive for all of them. After numerous ultimatums she threw Peter out in the late 1940s and went on to raise her children, my first cousins Raymond and Sharon, on her own. That was the point at which contact with the New Zealand family ceased.

Peter Crawley, meantime, had an erratic career. Initially he managed to secure senior and well paid work on defence contracts – making jets for Douglas Aircraft in California and missiles for Northrop and Lockheed. But each time drink affected his reliability and behaviour and he lost his job. Eventually he was blackballed by both the aircraft and automobile industries and banned from defence contracts. He was forced back to jobs on the factory floor. He married twice more, once to an African-American woman. He died of a heart attack in Florida, aged sixty-four. Pauline brought his body back to Michigan for burial alongside Raymond, who had been killed five years earlier.

Considering that they had gone to Detroit to find work and security in the expanding car industries, the automobile exacted a terrible toll on the family: Great-grandmother Crawley killed by the hit-and-run driver in 1927; Pauline's father killed in a crash; my first cousin

Raymond killed in a head-on collision in 1969; my other cousin Sharon permanently injured in a similar accident. Even my uncle had a serious smash the year before he died, and his second wife Catherine and her father were killed when the car she was driving left the road.

My aunt in Detroit was left with a lonely and painful legacy: a lost husband, a lost son, a permanently disabled daughter, and grandchildren who were taken to another state after Raymond was killed and forbidden to communicate with her. And yet she was and is a courageous and coping woman, and meeting her and remaining in communication with her has been a source of inspiration.

At one level, the narrative I have outlined is the story of a single migrant family. At another level, however, it is consistent with a pattern of mutations that certain *kinds* of migrants encounter in their relations with countries and cultures of origin; and in relations with their new, host countries.

The first generation – those who actually plan and carry out the migration – are well aware, sometimes painfully so, of where they have come from. But they concentrate their attention and energies on getting established and accepted in their adoptive country. Very often they suppress feelings and information about what they have left behind and hide those feelings from children and grandchildren – because the factors which led to migration were hurtful and stressful, and to make adjustment to the new society less troublesome.

The second generation, the children of migrants, usually want to merge as wholly as possible with the host community. Often they conceal how recent is the arrival of their family in the new country. If parents have accents or language difficulties, children are inclined to find this a source of embarrassment, a badge of not truly belonging in a society to which the children of migrants want strongly to belong. In my father's case, being a New Zealander required an 'ordinary'

New Zealand background, an 'ordinary' home, an 'ordinary' family life. Because he believed he had none of these things, he blocked out recollection of his actual past and had no inclination to share it with anybody, including his own mother and his children.

It is most often the third generation of migrants that is aware of the ancestral silence beyond the grandparents and becomes curious about it. The third generation has none of the acute preoccupations about 'getting established' and 'belonging' that worried grandparents and parents. They know that they are, by location and experience, New Zealanders. But in an increasingly secular world they may be aware of a cultural and spiritual vacuum, and part of that vacuum may derive from an ignorance of what lies higher on the rungs of their genealogical ladder.

I would surmise that all these factors are made more acute in New Zealand by the spectacle of a renaissance of Maori culture and identity occurring in full sight and sound of Pakeha New Zealand; and by the unmistakeable evidence that, as far as tangata whenua are concerned, a knowledge of who *they* are and where they have come from has made them strong and assertive – has transformed, in fact, what most Pakeha formerly regarded as the negative experience of being Maori into a profoundly positive one.

What I have been describing, of course, is merely a single thread in a complex and tightly woven pattern of migrant culture. But for me, following that thread to its source through a Minotaur tunnel of silence, darkness and potential wrong turnings has brought me closer to an answer to that most basic question we ask ourselves: 'Who or what am I?'

The first and the most prosaic result of the search is a negative accomplishment: the absence of what was formerly a blank page on one side of the family genealogy. To state that more positively, I now know biographical details about ancestors back to great-great-grandparents on both sides of the family who derive from villages in Ireland prior to the Famine. To put it yet another way, I now have beginnings of stories to which I formerly had only middles and endings.

These rediscovered ancestors now have names, physical features in the case of those of whom I was able to find photographs, and particular places of origin that I now have the option of visiting. I also know a little of the character and mannerisms of some of these people, ingredients that have gone into the present generation's makeup and – like eye colouring, odd-shaped noses or a striking kind of glare – reappear in varying proportions among my brother and sisters, cousins, nieces and nephews.

There is more to be gained than even that, however. A specific knowledge of one's antecedents and where they have come from, and in what circumstances, provides a sense of confidence and continuity with which to confront the uncertainties of life in the twenty-first century AD. An appreciation of the enormity of obstacles which forebears managed to surmount and surpass is a source of personal strength and stamina in dealing with contemporary attitudes ('if my ancestors could do *that*, I can do *this*'). For those who value it, such knowledge is an antidote to that fear expressed by Edmund Burke that, for all our noisiness and our darting and our busyness, humankind may amount to little more than flies of a summer.

2.

Being Pakeha

1991

Among some New Zealanders the word 'Pakeha' has come to be seen as a term of abuse. In 1990, a National Party backbencher claimed that its root meaning was 'long white pig' and that its continued use was an insult to all New Zealanders of European descent. He called for the word to be banned, without making it clear how such a prohibition could be imposed. This call was supported by some leader writers and columnists, and by rather more writers of letters to the editor. Do such people have a case? Is the word pejorative?

The meaning and first use of the word lie so far back in Maori oral tradition that we shall probably never know its precise origin. Assemble a group of knowledgeable kaumatua to debate the question, as I have done, and you will get a variety of answers: that the word is derived from keha, or flea; from the expression for white clay; from pakepakeha, the mythological fairy people with pale skins; from the same word meaning outlandish; or that it was a corruption of the expression that Maori heard most frequently from the first sailor and sealer and whaler visitors: 'Bugger ya!'

Most Maori scholars find the pakepakeha derivation, referring to white skins, most likely. We do know that the word was in common use as early as 1824, which was when Dumont d'Urville used it in an unpublished manuscript as a Maori word to describe Europeans.

What can be said with more precision is that, as an adjective, the word now denotes non-Maori and usually Western or European phenomena; and that as a noun it refers to people of predominantly European descent. It *can* be used as a pejorative expression, as can the word Maori in some contexts ('Maori car', 'Maori time'). But most often it is not. In common use 'Pakeha' is simply a descriptive word applied to non-Polynesian people and things in New Zealand that derive originally from outside New Zealand – most often from Europe, and even more specifically, because of the nature of our history, from the United Kingdom.

To me it is the obvious word to describe such things. 'New Zealand' is too general a term, because there is not a single coherent culture that gives all New Zealanders a shared vision of themselves and their place in the world. 'European' is inadequate because – as I have suggested – many of the things called Pakeha are several generations removed from Europe. 'Caucasian' is inaccurate and inappropriate. 'Tauiwi' means a strange tribe or foreign race, aliens, a truly offensive term for people who have been here for over a hundred and fifty years. And 'non-Maori' is a negative definition, indicating what something is *not* rather than what it is.

'Pakeha', on the other hand, is an indigenous New Zealand expression that denotes things that belong to New Zealand via one major stream of its heritage: people, manners, values and customs that are not exclusively Polynesian. But it also denotes *things that are no longer simply European*. It denotes people and things that *derive* from abroad but that, through the transformations of history and geography, through their new characteristics and combinations, are now unlike their sources and antecedents.

Some obvious examples: the music of Vivaldi and Bach is European, not Pakeha; the music of Jenny McLeod and From Scratch is Pakeha, not European. The stories of Chekhov and Roald Dahl are European; those of Owen Marshall and John Cranna Pakeha. The films *Diva* and *Fitzcarraldo* are European; *Smash Palace* and *Vigil* are Pakeha. And so on. There is ample sufficiency of cultural features and products that have been so transformed in New Zealand as to be distinguishable from their origins.

Let me stress this. To say that something is Pakeha in character is not to diminish its New Zealand-ness, as some people claim in the periodic controversies over the use of the word. It is to emphasise and refine it. It is to achieve a more detailed and more focused definition of something in New Zealand. If I say that Mira Szaszy, Sonja Davies and Michael Jones are New Zealanders, then I am telling the truth. But if I say that Mira Szaszy is a Maori New Zealander, Sonja Davies a Pakeha New Zealander and Michael Jones is a Samoan New Zealander, then I am communicating information about those people that is more specific, more interesting and more useful.

The next thing to consider is whether or not there is such as thing as Pakeha culture in New Zealand. By culture, of course, I am not referring simply to the arts, nor more especially to the 'high' arts, as some people do when they use the term. I refer to the basis of the relationship between the individual and society, the values and rituals through which people perceive and feel their identity; and by which society accepts them – for culture, by its nature, is both inclusive and exclusive.

It includes the arts, of course, the music, painting and literature to which I have made reference, and which is perhaps most easily distinguishable from the cultural expressions of other countries. But it also includes experience of history, it includes going to school and what is taught there, going to church, playing rugby or netball, membership of the Returned Services Association, and so on. It includes using language in a manner that is not quite the same as the manner in which that same language is used elsewhere. And it includes habits and customs that also differ from those in other countries, even closely related countries.

In these senses, it is readily apparent that Pakeha New Zealand and Pakeha New Zealanders do have a culture. It may not be coherent or tightly cohesive. Few of its ingredients may be exclusive. But the combinations in which those ingredients come together are exclusive. And this is most often revealed by the manner in which Pakeha New Zealanders are capable of closing ranks against people from other countries and cultures – the Aussies, the Poms, the Japs and the Frogs, to use the language of exclusion. It is less discreditably illustrated by the experience of New Zealanders outside New Zealand.

More and more New Zealanders are travelling and have travelled. That process turns a minority of them into expatriates, blurring their sense of identity and belonging. The majority, however, see with the perspective of distance contours in New Zealand life – especially Pakeha New Zealand life – that are not so visibly apparent at home.

Let me quote again from *Being Pakeha*, because the experience I describe there is one that is common to my generation:

> The effect of my first year away from New Zealand was to make me feel more, not less, a New Zealander. I became more deeply conscious of my roots in my own country because I had experienced their absence. I missed physical things, like empty land and seascapes,

> driftwood fires, bush, New Zealand birdsong. And I missed common perspectives with Maori and Pakeha New Zealanders: the short-cuts to communication that people from the same cultures share in accepted reference points, recognised allusions, a similar sense of comparison, contrast and incongruity, a peculiar sense of humour. I had resented being ignored by some Europeans and patronised by others, diminished in their eyes simply because of the place in which I was born; being made to feel that the centre of the universe was *there*, and that what was happening on the periphery, where I came from, was of little consequence.
>
> All this contributed to a conviction that New Zealanders, for all their faults, had virtues that were precious: an unwillingness to be intimidated by the new, the formidable, or class systems; trust in situations where there would otherwise be none; compassion for the underdog; a sense of responsibility for people in difficulty; not undertaking to do something without seeing it through – what Dan Davin called 'a kind of power behind the scrum that one felt was lacking in one's sometimes more fastidious English colleagues'; a lesser degree of racial prejudice (though not an absence) than that apparent in many other parts of the world. With the perspective of distance, New Zealanders seem to have gone much further towards developing cultural traits than they had at home, where one was far more conscious of variety and disagreement. I also became more aware of the value of my Maori associations; of what New Zealand would lose by way of its modest sense of antiquity, ritual, poetry, grace and humour if it were left solely with an Anglo-Saxon heritage.

This raises another point that interests me. While Maori are Maori and Pakeha are Pakeha, each has been influenced by the other and had his or her culture shaped decisively by the other. One essential ingredient of Pakeha-ness, as far as I am concerned, is contact with and being affected by Maori things: Maori concepts, Maori values, Maori language and Maori relationships. As I also said in *Being Pakeha*, the Maori presence here has given the land on which we live a historical echo, a resonance it would entirely lack had the Maori not *been* here first, *lived* here first and *named* things first. Whenever I go to a new place or visit a familiar one, I instinctively look first for the shapes on the land and the middens that indicate where the first inhabitants of that place chose to make their home and gather food. I am drawn to and comforted by the psychic residue of their presence.

The existence of the tangata whenua has also put me in touch with symbols that may arise out of the whole of human collective consciousness, but here are Maori and therefore indigenously New Zealand in idiom. It has exposed me to concepts – the mauri of people and places, tapu, mana, whenuatanga, whanaungatanga – that, again, have their roots in this part of the world, but are also universal in occurrence, value and application.

My brush with all these things doesn't make me Maori. But they are an essential part of the experience that makes me Pakeha – experience I could not have had access to in any other part of the world. For a growing number of people, even those who react negatively to the encounter, Pakeha-ness embraces some experience of Maori history, habits, values and expectations.

And this leads me to the final major point I wish to make. If one recognises the existence of the evolving Pakeha culture of which I speak, and if one accepts that it is a phenomenon that could only accrete in New Zealand from the Maori, European and wider human ingredients that history has cast up on these shores – then what we are acknowledging here is not something foreign: it is a *second indigenous New Zealand culture.*

For that is what Pakeha culture is for me, and what it is becoming for a growing number of New Zealanders whose primary loyalty is to

New Zealand. It is not an indigenous culture that displaces or supplants that of the tangata whenua. It is in a symbiotic relationship to Maoritanga. But it is as important as Maoritanga; and it *is* being and *will* be fed as much by its own memories and traditions as Maoritanga is by *its* past (one has only to think of the impact of the national recollection of the Gallipoli experience). And – because it will increasingly nourish and sustain Pakeha people and enable more and more of them to feel that they truly belong in this part of the world – it will be a vital component in the process of Maori-Pakeha accommodation. Because Pakeha people will cease to feel threatened by the enlarging Maori presence in New Zealand when they have begun to feel whole and to feel secure. The proponents of the white backlash are those who are not whole, and who feel anything but secure.

It is largely these people, I believe, who fear and object to the word Pakeha. Not being wholly confident as to who or what they are, they resent being labelled and (as they see it) defined by another culture and another language. And, although they lay claim to New Zealand-ness in preference to Pakeha identity, by that very fact – by their rejection of an indigenous New Zealand term – they are expressing a stronger commitment to their European culture of origin than to the country in which they live.

I am fully in agreement with Ranginui Walker on this point: use of the word Pakeha is part of the process by which the descendants of European colonists achieve a New Zealand identity.

I have conducted most of this exploration on a personal level. Let me close in an equally personal way – which will, I hope, illustrate some of the complexities inherent in what I have been saying; but also the truths and the grounds for optimism.

I live part of each year in a rural community on the Coromandel Peninsula. There, local Maori families are largely in favour of mining and coastal subdivision and the general concept of 'development'. Pakeha members of that community, who derive their livelihood from farming, horticulture, teaching, or from activities such as writing and pottery, are the ones who are wrestling with the local council and the planning tribunal to preserve an unmodified estuary and coastline, in order to retain features of scientific, historical, recreational and aesthetic value; and it is Pakeha who are trying to get legislative and planning protection for pa sites, urupa and other wahi tapu.

What is of most interest to me in this situation is not what some would see – and do see – as the incongruous position of the iwi Maori – they, after all, are not tangata whenua ('Those are not our bones and they're nothing to do with us,' as one elder said to me when I tried to get support for reserving an old burial ground); and, most importantly, they see development of the industrial and mining kind as likely to bring long-term income and job security for their children and grand-children, allowing them to continue to live on family land instead of having to join the chain migration to the cities.

That is of less concern to me here than the reasons why a group of Pakeha people should become militant about the preservation of clean water, native trees and birds, sources of kai moana and historic sites – when one remembers that it was the introduction of pastoral farming, industrialisation and the cash economy by Europeans that put these features under stress in the first place.

For some, particularly for the absentee owners, the weekend visitors, I have no doubt that their support of conservation values is directed at preserving an insulated playground of peace and cleanliness to which they can retreat from the stresses of Monday-to-Friday jobs in Queen Street glass towers. For others, though, particularly for those of us who actually live there, something else is going on. We are in the process of establishing a relationship with the land on which we live, and with the wider environment that surrounds us. We have moved from the belief that the land belongs to us to the feeling that we belong to the land. And we fear betrayal of that relationship if this same land is strip-mined, denuded of trees, or sealed off in asphalt, concrete and high-density housing.

Merita Mita said once that, for her, the difference between town and country was that air and land and water in the cities had become inorganic and lost their life force; whereas those in rural areas remained alive, retaining their mauri and offering something to which the human psyche could respond and relate. And that that relationship was a form of spirituality.

From a different direction, but one not uninfluenced by Maori concepts, I have arrived at a similar cosmology. 'All is seared with trade, bleared smeared with toil,' Gerard Manley Hopkins wrote. 'And wears man's smudge, and bears man's smell. The soil is bare now, nor can foot feel being shod.' That is an expression of the loss that I fear if the march of development/corporatisation/industrialisation is allowed to proceed unchecked. It is not simply the loss of an aesthetic outlook; it is the loss of relationship with the planet that has spawned us.

An explanation of why I should feel this way is perhaps most easily and most superficially derived from a series of recent items in my curriculum vitae. But I am aware that, beyond recent experience, I am seeing and acting as a consequence of values imprinted on me in childhood. And, beyond those, I am acting out a version of my grandparents' vision of life away from greasy cobblestones and sandstone tenements and grimy mines and mills.

I can even go further and believe that I am influenced by race memories of great-great-grandparents on the west coast of Ireland, planting and cultivating and worshipping in view of the sea high over Clew Bay in County Mayo; or of those other great-great-grandparents working their crofts in Easter Ross alongside Cromarty Firth. These, for me, are the recollections, myths and dreams that seep down to me from my ancestry and which stamp the present unconscious with habits, values and expectations.

And for me, as much as for any Maori person, the songs of *this* land are still to be heard: those of Tangaroa from the beaches, Tane Mahuta in the forest, Tawhirimatea from the hillside. I hear them because they vibrate from the ethos of the land, and because I am open to them. I hear them too because they are in harmony with those rhythms, patterns and continuities that come to me from my Pakeha, Celtic and European past.

They heal me, they uplift me, they nourish me. They give me a sense each day of being born anew. They are an integral part – perhaps the *most* integral part – of my being a New Zealander, of being Pakeha.

3.

Contradictions

1988

I can't recall when I first became aware of concepts such as masculinity and femininity. Having sisters, one six years older than me, one six years younger, I knew about male and female differences from an early age. And playing doctors and nurses with a slightly older school mate – she was seven, I was six – made my knowledge of anatomical differences explicit.

Throughout my primary school years at Paremata, the messages I must have learned at home were reinforced, however. Girls did some things, boys did others. Boys were allowed to be rough with each other – bullrush, rugby or just wrestling in the playground – but not with girls. Girls had cooking lessons, we went to woodwork and metalwork at an adjacent school. And, greatest difference of all, learned by observation and anticipation: girls eventually become mothers, who stayed at home to look after their husband and children; boys became fathers who drove the car, went out to work, visited the pub or the club sometimes on the way home and worked in the garden at weekends. These were things we saw at home; everything that was said at school indicated that they were no more than God's will and the natural order of things. Weren't the Holy Family an example? Joseph working as a carpenter, Mary as homemaker, and Jesus following in Joseph's footsteps for the first thirty years of his life?

Our home life was close and harmonious. My mother was a full-time mother. She fed us, she clothed us, she played with us, she gave us kisses and cuddles. She directed her attention to resolving conflict rather than worrying about it. She was at home when, breakfasted and carrying our lunch and playlunch, we left to walk to school; she was there when we returned in the afternoon. Sometimes in summer she would pick us up from school and take us for a swim on Plimmerton Beach. While we were at school she washed the dishes and clothes, ironed, vacuumed floors, planned meals, bought food, and occasionally played Canasta with other house-bound women in our street.

The men's routine was very different but just as universal in our neighbourhood. My father left for work in the city long before we set out for school (he faced a half-hour train trip or a longer car ride). He worked all day in an office doing things I didn't understand, but which 'made money' and 'paid the bills'. The only specific indication I had of some of the requirements of his career was the fact that we always ate Weetbix and filled the car with Europa petrol, because the companies that produced these products were his clients.

My father usually came home from work at about 6 p.m. We knew when his appearance was imminent because my mother helped us tidy away our toys, drawings, comics and books. There was to be no 'mess' when he walked through the door. We also had to be quieter, my mother said, because he would be tired after a 'hard day at the office'. Coming through the door my father would kiss my mother, kiss us, pour them a drink, and they would talk about their respective days (though my father rarely discussed work). Then my mother served dinner. Sometimes, though, especially on Friday nights, my father came home later, after we had eaten; and on these occasions he was more gregarious than he was on other nights. Occasionally this seemed to please my mother, who joined in whatever impromptu fun developed, showing 8-mm cartoons from Kodak, drawing pictures for us, playing skittles, or pretending to be 'the Gilli Gilli Man' who had amused New Zealand troops and sailors with sleight of hand in Arab ports during the war. At other such times my mother seemed constrained and we were put to bed early.

Some of my mother's 'quiet' times were those when my father brought other people home late with him. These late-night 'uncles' always seemed to have had more to drink than my father. They were louder and more demonstrative. This too did not please my mother. One such visitor was Denis Glover, who worked for a time at my father's advertising agency and whose voice sounded – in Brian Bell's phrase – like 'an Oxford-trained circular saw'.

One morning after Denis had stayed overnight in the spare room, my mother sent me in with a cup of tea to wake him. I was surprised to find that the picture of the Sacred Heart, which normally hung on the bedroom wall, was face down on the carpet. 'Did the picture fall down, Mr Glover?' I asked politely. 'What?' said Denis, puckering his face into an estimation of the extent of the previous evening's damage. Then he exploded with relief. 'Oh no,' he said. 'I *put* it there. I felt bad enough as it was without having bleeding Jesus reproach me.'

Midweek, my father had quite different reasons for sometimes arriving home late. His work for voluntary organisations was extensive and something which, as a result of his example, I regarded as a natural thing for men to do. He viewed the obligation of community service as self-evident: 'Where you take something out you must always put something back.' Hence he devoted much of what would otherwise have been free time over the years to bodies concerned with the welfare of servicemen and former servicemen, as he did later to organisations such as the Cancer Society, the Navy League and the Duke of Edinburgh Award scheme. It was because of his example that I felt a similar sense of obligation to become involved in relevant professional activities from the time I left school.

A second and related trait of my father's which I regarded as 'manly', and which influenced me just as strongly, was his absolute commitment on matters on which he had given his word, even if the execution of that commitment turned out to be difficult or disruptive of his private life. He never let us back out of agreements we had made, at home, at school or elsewhere, just as he himself never let anybody down once he had undertaken to do something. Your word, as the adage had it, was your bond.

The third thing about my father that I came to associate with masculinity – but which I remember witnessing long before I had any concept of masculinity – was the courtliness he displayed towards women, including my mother. He was sensitive and attentive to them at all times. He raised his hat to them in the street, offered his seat on the bus or the train and always got to his feet when they came into a room. The feeling I acquired from witnessing this behaviour – by osmosis rather than from explicit discussion – was that men were to respect and protect women and treat them at all times with more gentle consideration than men gave to men. My father's dealings with other men, on the other hand, his friends and acquaintances, tended to be direct and characterised by robust bonhomie.

Most weekends my father worked outside while my mother prepared food and did housework. He had elaborate gardens: he cut lawns, grew vegetables, planted trees and flowers, built boulder walls and permanent barbecues. He did all his own handiwork, painting the house when necessary, repairing roofs, spouting and anything else that broke, constructing shelves. When we were small we were allowed to 'help' – gathering up grass, sitting on top of the wheelbarrow when he took cuttings to the compost heap. As we became older, however, gardening became a solitary occupation for my father, except when he stopped to share morning and afternoon teas with us, featuring scones or cakes which my mother had just baked. Much later, when I was an adolescent, I was recruited to cut lawns, dig the vegetable garden and wash the car, also on my own. It did not seem like fun.

The times I most enjoyed with my father were the occasions when we went off together to look for and at birds round the Pauatahanui arm of Paremata Harbour. These excursions enhanced my awareness of and love of nature – of unpolluted earth and water, of the life of plants and birds. I also enjoyed the companionship: the feeling that we were related and close and that I was special to him and safe with him. The frequency of such expeditions diminished as I grew older and I missed them.

Another opportunity my father enjoyed that my mother seemed not to have was the odd weekend away with friends, duck-shooting, rabbit-shooting or fishing. These were boisterous affairs, what we saw of them, much alcohol being loaded into the cars along with rifles, guns, ammunition and fishing rods. They also resulted in food, though it was my mother who had to pluck birds and cook carcases. We could tell that she didn't really approve of these expeditions. But she did not (as far as I know) try to stop them. They were seasonal and hence infrequent.

The most important thing I was aware of that men did and women did not (on the whole) was fight wars. In *New Zealanders at War* I wrote that, after the First and Second World Wars, the following generations in New Zealand 'did not need to be told that the Angel of Death had passed over the land: they had heard the beating of its wings'. For me, this was no exaggeration. My father's father had been killed in France in 1915. My maternal grandmother displayed a photograph of her favourite cousin, Cuthbert, killed in the same war at about the same time and place. Next door to us lived Mrs Hornig, who had lost her husband in World War One and her only son, Colin, in North Africa in World War Two. Sepia photographs of young men in khaki, frozen in youth and with what seemed like an expectation of death on their faces, were among the icons of my youth. They had faded 'Flanders poppies' wedged in the corners of the frames.

I had closer reminders of war. My father's photographs of his four years in the Royal Navy and two in the Royal New Zealand Navy. His medals worn on Anzac Day dawn parades and on other occasions – such as the Government House garden party for the Queen – that required uniform. And there were his reminiscences of war, which usually emerged when he had old comrades-in-arms (or in-ships) at home. He had been stoic, brave and decorated for his bravery and he was reluctant to talk about the torrid features of war, however.

Our neighbourhood abounded in veterans. Down the road was an elderly man I liked to visit, Tiny Mann, whose family business had been responsible for the unforgettable slogan painted on the sloping roof of the woolshed at Plimmerton: 'LADIES WEAR MANN'S SHOES'. Tiny had fought in the South African War and he showed me photographs of men on horseback, wearing slouch hats and bandoliers, looking more like Mexican bandits than New Zealand troops galloping across the veldt.

Professor Bob Monro, another neighbour, had fought in France in World War One and was present at the courts martial of New Zealand, Australian and British troops at Étaples. He rejected the camaraderie of the RSA, but he loved talking about 'the war'. And Jim Crabbe, a rough-talking, hard-drinking ex-farmer who used to take my father fishing, had been wounded in France in the same war and left for dead. He had been rescued by nuns from a pile of unburied bodies and nursed back to health. But his injuries bequeathed him with a lifelong limp. My step-grandfather Jimmy was another veteran of Flanders. When he died, he was eulogised at the graveside in the soldiers' cemetery at Karori by a wisp of an RSA representative, who balanced precariously against the gale on one leg and one crutch. He threw a paper poppy towards the coffin but the wind carried it away.

All this was a constant reminder to me that, within living memory, each generation preceding mine had had to go to war in defence of freedom and the British way of life. Glumly, I accepted that that too would be my fate. I wasn't sure that I would survive (my father had, my grandfather had not). But I was far more worried about whether or not I would show courage under fire. The only time my physical bravery had been put to the test was at the dental clinic, and I had proved such an abject coward there that I feared for my ability to uphold the family (and the national) honour.

The nuns at school made it clear to us that the next war would be started by 'the Communists': those who had killed Catholics in Eastern Europe and slaughtered missionaries in China. Father Peyton came from Ireland to conduct the great Rosary Crusade in 1954 and told us that the expansionist creeds of the Soviet Union and China would sweep the Western World and bring about a new Dark Age if we did not say the rosary daily and devoutly. This produced new anxieties to trouble me in bed at night: if we were prepared to fight bravely but insufficient people said the rosary, would we lose World War Three? If we said the rosary instead of fighting, would fighting prove unnecessary? The adult world was complicated. And frightening.

Taught by nuns, we lacked male role models at school; apart, that is, from the priests who took us for religious instruction and heard our confessions. Some of those priests, like Father Jeremiah McGrath, were tall, forthcoming, muscular and 'manly'. Others were short, slight and shy. Father McGrath was the dominant figure. His physique seemed protective, his certitudes banished doubt, and his Irish humour warmed us (he called my parents 'Your Majesties' and I was 'the Little Prince'). But there was a contradiction in his behaviour. He didn't drink alcohol. He wore a Pioneer's badge, which indicated he had taken a vow of life-long total abstinence. This presented me with one of my first examples of antithesis, a syllogism that didn't work: men drink alcohol; Father McGrath is a man, a powerful man; but he doesn't drink. What was to be concluded? I didn't know.

Another man who provided a role model outside the family was Cliff Porter, captain of the 1924 All Blacks, the Invincibles. 'Uncle Cliff', as I knew him, had no sons. He liked having a boy around to trot beside him and listen to his tales of valour on the rugby field while he cut and rolled his bowling green. I heard all about Mark Nicholls, Bert Cooke, the Brownlies and George Nepia. I heard why Cliff had been dropped from the crucial 1928 tour of South Africa. As a special treat he took me into 'the bach', a cottage next to his house which was a kind of museum. Rugby photographs covered the walls, boxes bulged with faded All Black jerseys, caps with tassels and disintegrating newspaper clippings. I knew then, with a kind of awe, that Cliff, like Edmund Hillary, was a great New Zealander. I realised later that 'the bach' was the place to which his wife exiled him when he had been drinking or when he wanted to drink with his cronies. Again there was a conflict: 'manly' men drank alcohol, but this was apparently not approved of by wives (nor, it seemed, by priests). Another neighbour highlighted this disapproval even further by throwing plates and cups at her husband when he had been drinking with Cliff, a real-life realisation of the Jiggs and Maggie cartoons we read daily in the *Evening Post*.

Our convent school was not sufficiently large to muster a rugby team, though Father Kavanagh tried once, enlisting two of the nuns at first and second five-eighths for practice. Apart from Cliff Porter's stories and trophies, therefore, I had little direct contact with the game until secondary school. But the 1956 Springbok visit dominated my life for the duration of the tour. Encouraged by Cliff, I cut out every item and photograph about the South Africans and their local opponents from newspapers, the *Free Lance* and the *Auckland Weekly News*. They were pasted carefully into a large scrapbook. I listened to every weekend game the Springboks played outside Wellington. I gave Mrs Balloti, the parish priest's housekeeper, shortened versions of games' commentaries, complete with Winston McCarthy's signature phrases. The Wellington games – against Wellington, New Zealand Universities and the All Blacks in the second test – we watched with other schools from an enclosure beside the southern touch-line at Athletic Park. I never forgot the roar that went up when the players in black emerged from the tunnel under the main stand. The charisma generated by a large crowd watching live rugby is the closest thing to raw nationalism I have experienced.

It was secondary school, boarding school, that exposed me to the full force of rugby culture, however, and to the dilemmas of sex; both seemed linked in our minds and behaviour. Returning in buses from matches away from college we would sing. Not the 'approved' and harmless songs, handed out on cyclostyled sheets; but the ones that were part of the school's oral tradition, passed underground from one generation of students to another. The most popular went to the tune of 'Mademoiselle from Armentières':

We're the boys from over the hill
Silverstream
We're the boys from over the hill
Silverstream

We're the boys from over the hill
We give the girls a helluva thrill
Inky pinky Silverstream.

Most of us had never been sufficiently intimate with members of the opposite sex to give them any kind of thrill. The songs were in effect variations on the school haka: expressions of school spirit, of bravado, or male clubbiness, of exulting our interests over those of outsiders. The next verse went:

The cops have warned us often enough
At Silverstream
The cops have warned us often enough
At Silverstream
The cops have warned us often enough
We couldn't give a tuppenny stuff
Inky pinky Silverstream.

We did know, partly instinctively and partly because of communications from recent old boys belonging to Catholic clubs throughout the country, that playing rugby hard and winning were associated with swaggering in front of women. And it was a matter of high prestige to be able to point to girlfriends following one's progress (however uncomprehendingly) in the course of a Saturday afternoon game. Playing and winning were also associated with alcohol in the world outside, though that was rarely smuggled on to our buses. When somebody did manage to get some beer, it was appropriated by the yahoos in the back seat, who knew that what was expected was to drink as much as possible as quickly as possible, while showing as little effect for it as possible. The remainder of the bus looked on with a mixture of disapproval and envy.

The only element in this equation that the school actively encouraged was playing rugby hard. It *was* a sport; but it was not *just* a sport. It was also an arena in which we displayed manly qualities by being fearless, by going into the rucks hard, by tackling hard, by going down on the ball in the face of on-rushing opponents, by never giving up. We upheld the school's reputation by winning and diminished it by losing. There was no Olympic nonsense about taking part and the trying being more important than the winning. We had to win. And we were dressed down severely if we did not.

I had an ambivalent relationship with rugby, as I did with the other major ingredients of male culture, alcohol and sex. In my first two years at secondary school I didn't play the game, ostensibly because of the effect of breaking my leg skiing. In fact, away from Cliff Porter's influence, I had become contemptuous of the spectacle of 'muddied oafs at the goal' and of the fact that the school motto, 'Take courage: be a man', was presented to us as something to be proved most often on the sports field. 'Manliness' was explicitly associated with physical toughness if not violence, with stamina and emotional control. In contrast, I used the time allocated to sport to read poetry and novels. This cast me as an outsider. Contempt for the game remained, but I did not enjoy being characterised as 'a swot'; nor being excluded from the easy camaraderie that those who played together displayed on and off the field. They had the masonic intimacy of men who had fought together in a war: they trusted each other, confided in each other, shared jokes economically and draped their arms unselfconsciously around one another's shoulders.

In my third year I shifted to another school, St Pat's Silverstream, and I chose to play the game; or, more accurately, I failed to resist the assumption that I would. To my dismay, I played abysmally. I was unfit, overweight, tentative about tackling, and frightened of being hurt, and I off-loaded the ball as soon as possible if it found its way miraculously into my hands. I was relegated to the lowest second-grade team with the halt, the lame and the blind, with the obese and the incurably clumsy. This was coached by the one priest in the school universally acknowledged as knowing nothing about rugby. We didn't try, and we lost every match. We didn't enjoy that. By the end of the season I was determined to lift my game and my grade the following year, to escape the humiliation of the company and the match record.

At the beginning of the next season I graduated to the first grade, because of my size. But I was despatched to trials with the D team, on account of my performance the previous year. Humiliation persisted. I was set upon breaking out of this pariah group, which was despised by the rest of the school almost as much as non-players. So I adopted the same approach I used in any other activity when I wanted to succeed. I prepared, I thought about tactics, and I applied myself single-mindedly to the games themselves. In practical terms this meant long early-morning runs to develop stamina, use of weights in the gymnasium to increase my arm, shoulder and leg-power, secret practice on the scrum machine, hurling myself at the tackling bag, reading books on rugby strategies, and playing on the field as if I were demented.

This application was rewarded. My game was transformed. I built sufficient stamina to be first to the ball and to stay near it for the full eighty minutes of play. I tackled like a maniac, launching myself full-length into the air and crashing the thighs of my opposite numbers, who always came down; sometimes they fell before I hit them, out of sheer terror. I found too that if I put my head down low and ran hard at the opposition, ball under my arm, they parted like the Red Sea. Within weeks I was scoring tries virtually unchallenged and I was stopping others doing the same. The feeling of power and satisfaction was short-lived, however. My newly acquired dominance was dependent on the opposition being pathetic. I was now playing above my grade.

And so, after congratulating me on a dramatic improvement, coaches consulted and moved me up the ladder. I was placed in 1B, under the eye of the most fanatic trainer in the school, Father Gus Hill. His method of coaching was a combination of encouragement and character assassination. He made me a tight-head prop and I found myself playing hard against people who played as hard or harder.

As we trained, Father Hill kept up a litany of comment and abuse: 'Stop dancing round like Mata Hari'; 'Don't be a great ninny'; and, once, belting me alternately on both cheeks, 'Get mad, King, get mad.' I did. We played. We won. It was exhilarating. Girls came to watch. And, after matches, I lay in the infirmary with an infra-red lamp on my bruises while my coach told me how well I had played. I was part of the masonic brotherhood. I simmered with satisfaction and sang on the buses with as much gusto as anybody.

Perhaps we associated sex with sport because our adolescent rugby careers unfolded at the same time as our sexuality. And, although this was never made clear to us at the time, one of the reasons for placing so much emphasis on sport was to sublimate sexual impulses. An idle mind was the devil's workshop, and so was an idle body. Paradoxically, although it may have reduced the incidence of self-abuse, the machismo swagger that seemed part of being superbly fit and winning games also nudged us towards exaggerated feelings of sexual competence and fantasies about how we would conquer women when the opportunities presented themselves.

The opportunities, however, were few, mainly confined to highly supervised school dances. For most of us, having spent two years learning to dance under the tutelage of Miss Margaret O'Connor, practising with male partners our own age, the experience of finally holding a female in our arms on the dance floor was devastating. We sweated (in white gloves), we stumbled, we stuttered. The carefully prepared conversational gambits evaporated. I remember one of the most boastful hoons in my class being deflated by a simple exchange with a partner several inches taller than him. 'My name's Trafford,' he began. 'You must be joking,' she said and shrieked with laughter. The scourge of the rugby buses and intermediate boxing champion was unable to utter another word all evening. To bolster our confidence and (as we imagined) to impress our partners, we passed around an MG key-ring to drop on the floor casually as we pulled out a handkerchief.

As we got older and became second- and then third-year dance veterans, this aspect of our lives became more comfortable. Those of us who were lucky formed friendships with some of our partners, which made the dances part of a wider context of association – along with letters, phone calls and movies in the holidays – and therefore less traumatic. But there was always tension between friendship and sex, and between the tenets of our education and the expectations of the male culture of which we were part.

Most of us would admit privately that we valued friendship over sex. And yet sex, raw sex, was a source of insatiable interest: because of our appetites and because most of us hadn't experienced intercourse. Those who claimed to have done – and boasted about it, describing lurid details to wide-eyed audiences down the river, away from priestly supervision – probably hadn't. Those who had, I suspect, didn't talk about it. A quiet, good-looking boy was in the toilet next to me one afternoon when a page of the letter he was reading fell and fluttered into my cubicle. I picked it up and began to look at it, thinking it was a message. It was a letter from a girl that was (to me) shockingly explicit in its eroticism. He asked for it back at once and never mentioned it again. Len, I judged, was in love, and 'doing it', and his very discretion added to my conviction that he had crossed the threshold.

The rest of us were trying to make sense out of conflicting messages. Our bodies wanted sex. Indeed, a friend said to me that the greatest tragedy he could imagine would be if the world was destroyed by nuclear holocaust before he had 'tried' intercourse. But our consciences and our explicit moral teaching told us that 'nice girls don't do it until they're married'. We tended to differentiate, then, between the 'nice' girls, our friends, the kind we would marry; and the 'bad' girls, the kind we would not marry but who would allow us to have sex. 'Allow us to have' was our view of it. All our education contributed to the notion that men wanted and needed sex; women either resisted or tolerated it, and hence were the ones who set the moral tone.

The impression, and the related division of womenkind into virgins/wives/mothers or whores, was unintentionally reinforced by the dedication of the order of priests that taught us to Mary, Mother of God, the Blessed Virgin herself. She was at all times held up as a model. And there was never any suggestion that *she* liked sex. On the contrary. She had conceived immaculately, via the Holy Spirit, thereby excluding the need for the grubby mechanisms of intercourse.

In addition, sex was almost always discussed in Christian Doctrine class as a problem, and heterosexual relations were lumped together with masturbation and homosexuality, with the implication that all were equally unfortunate. The message we took from this was that the impulses of the body were sinful and ought to be suppressed; and that no-sex was preferable to sex, celibacy a more virtuous option even than marriage. We accepted this at the time. But we still looked forward to sexual experience and would have grasped any opportunity that presented itself for experimentation. It was to be years before I reconciled these contradictory ideals and impulses within my own body and psyche.

I managed to avoid intensive personal encounters with alcohol – that other ingredient of manliness – until university. Here too the messages of upbringing and experience had been confusing. Manly men drink (Cliff Porter, Jim Crabbe); manly men *don't* drink (Father McGrath);

drinking in moderation is acceptable (school); drinking in moderation is acceptable for adults but not for adolescents (my parents).

In spite of my parents' familiarity with alcohol, I didn't drink at home. I wasn't offered a drink at home – and then only a small one – until I was nineteen. Instead, I began to drink alcohol at the homes of friends and at the dances and parties I began to attend after leaving school at seventeen. For a long time I had no problem with drink, nor was I worried by the conflicting views of society about its merits and evils. I was simply not interested. I occasionally drank moderately – beer, or more effete concoctions such as punch or horse's necks; alcohol was not crucial to my well-being nor to my having a good time.

I rarely went near a pub. The spectacle and smell of the public bar six o'clock swill – 'part stale beer, part disinfectant, part fart', as Jock Phillips has described it – revolted me; as did the pressure to buy 'rounds' and to drink rapidly and heavily at the risk of being labelled a 'piker'. I was not part of any drinking 'school', as were some of my male friends, particularly those involved in sport (the rumours at school had turned out to be true: most sportsmen, especially rugby players, drank heavily after the game; I had stopped playing rugby, reverting to skiing, and hence was not part of such a network).

My circumstances changed in my third year at university, however. I had become secretary of the students' association at Victoria, and was now living away from home. Most other members of the executive, male and female, *were* pub drinkers. With hangers-on they formed a group that met regularly at the Midland Hotel in Lambton Quay, on Friday evenings and on evenings before executive meetings. I began to attend: at first to be part of the group and to participate in the settling of student business that the formal meetings would merely ratify. After a short time, however, I began to enjoy the experience for its own sake.

Several things about it were new for me. One was the calibre of the company. I was surrounded by people who were articulate, politically aware and highly entertaining. The likes of Tony Hass, Murray Boldt and Trevor Crawford were so close to the New Zealand male stereotype (hard workers, hard players, hard drinkers, good fun and staunch mates) that I could scarcely believe they were real. They were. The camp followers, largely female, were a mixture of political activists and the twinset-and-pearls brigade, both groups gravitating for their own reasons towards where they assumed the power and the glamour lay. It was flattering to be an object of their attention.

The second novel factor was that I followed the example of most of the men and switched from draught beer to the more highly alcoholic export lagers. The consequence was that I became intoxicated quite quickly, and then drank only sparingly to sustain the level of euphoria. Everybody in the group seemed warm and hilarious, and we moved easily from there to executive meetings as a kind of fortified caucus who had already predetermined the outcome of deliberations; or, if it were Friday, to a cheap meal in a steak house or a coffee bar and on to a party.

It was a time of immense fun, of feeling that one belonged somewhere, of making useful things happen and of always having something to look forward to. But at the back of my mind there were reservations which came forward on subsequent days with the hangovers, and questioned whether this was me; whether – sober – I really felt comfortable about having done some of those things.

The piling into cars and being driven around by somebody intoxicated worried me in retrospect. So did our response at meetings to those who hadn't been drinking with us, and who consequently seemed earnest and boring. We sometimes treated them shabbily, saying for our own amusement things that were clever or hilarious rather than true or fair. When our president Chris Robertson arrived late and coldly sober and announced that he had been mounting birds at the museum, we were unable to stay straight-faced for the remainder of that meeting. Alcohol-warped judgements brought us close to endangering what reputations we had. Delivering one of our number to a reception for Rhodes Scholars (he had just become one), five of us stopped a taxi on Government House driveway, in view of Government House, and relieved ourselves into the vice-regal hydrangeas.

I came closest to disaster when, after a pub session followed by a party without a meal in between, I crashed at the flat of two female friends in Brougham Street. They were excessively tolerant. They lay me on a spare bed, removed my shoes, put a quilt over me and turned on a heater (it was winter). I was unconscious before the light went out. Somewhere in the early hours of the morning I woke, feeling paralysed and terribly ill. My mind functioned with agonising sluggishness. I couldn't remember who I was or where I was. I seemed to have no air in my lungs and when I made an effort to breathe more deeply I began to cough till I was choking. I managed to roll over away from the wall and saw a cameo like a scene from a film. There was a fire burning in the centre of a room, like some kind of Oriental shrine, and light flickered off the walls through a pall of smoke. I seemed to be watching it from a great distance.

It took me some seconds to realise what was happening. I had kicked the quilt off the bed and on to the bar heater. The quilt was now ablaze, and so possibly was the floor. The door and window were closed. I was close to suffocating from smoke inhalation. I had no subsequent recollection of the next few minutes. It seems I managed to get up, open the door, wrap up and pick up the burning quilt, get it into the bath next door and turn on the tap. Then I opened the window, called for help and passed out. The floor was scorched but miraculously not on fire. If it had been, the ancient wooden house would have incinerated rapidly.

The knowledge that I had come close to killing myself and endangering other lives was sufficiently sobering to bring about a change in lifestyle. I stopped pubbing. Indeed, for a time I stopped drinking alcohol. I saved the money I had spent previously on entertainment.

In another year I was married, living in Hamilton and holding my first full-time job. My difficulties in coming to terms with masculinity and masculine expectations were far from over, of course. The solution of one set of problems merely created others. But that is another chapter of another story . . .

4.

On Writing Maori History

A talk given as part of a panel discussion, Te Papa, 2001

Essentially, Maori history is the same as any other kind of history, in that it has the same purposes and the same methodology to achieve those purposes.

Those purposes are, of course, to illuminate the past – to tell us *how* things happened and *why* things happened. And in good history, they are carried out disinterestedly, objectively.

Good history is not written to enlarge the mana of Maori in general, or the mana of iwi, hapu or individuals. It's not written to score points, to put down one party and elevate another. It's not written to show that one people or one culture is inherently more virtuous or more sinful than another. All that is propaganda. History may be used or misused in propaganda. But it is not the same thing as propaganda.

History, as distinct from propaganda, seeks to show how things happened and why. And if it is good history it is characterised by accuracy, precision, balance and clarity.

As I've remarked on a previous occasion, while all good history has those characteristics, it's especially important for Maori history to have them. For two reasons:

One is that Maori history is an essential part of the process of claims against the Crown, and therefore susceptible to being used or to being condemned as propaganda. And if claims are to be successful, respected and enduring, they have to be shown to be founded in good history.

And the second is that some New Zealanders, those of the red-necked variety, are always waiting and hoping to be able to make the claim that Maori history is being sanitised to make Maori behaviour seem more virtuous than the behaviour and the performance of non-Maori. They must be given no grounds for doing so. Good Maori history must always be based on solid evidence, and on reasonable conclusions drawn from that evidence.

Shall I quote to you some examples of good and bad Maori history? Among the very best models I could cite would be Buddy Mikaere's splendid book on the South Island prophetic leader Te Maiharoa. A recent example is Ranginui Walker's magisterial and authoritative biography of Apirana Turupa Ngata. Another recent example is Paul Tapsell's riveting book on Pukaki, the Te Arawa tupuna and carving. Others would be almost all the Maori essays in the *Dictionary of New Zealand Biography*.

And bad examples? I have them but I am not going to name them. The laws of defamation are inhibiting. Suffice to say that none of them is written by members of tonight's panel.

Having talked about the congruence of Maori history and history in general, however, I should just mention one major respect in which the two genres differ.

In Western or non-Maori history, the subjects of history are seen as being the property of the community at large. When I wanted to write a biography of the wartime Prime Minister Peter Fraser, for example, I didn't need anybody's permission to do so. His life was public property. Similarly when I wrote a biography of Janet Frame, who is still living, I didn't need her permission to do so. I went and *got* her permission, because that made the process so much easier. But I didn't *have* to do so. And indeed another New Zealand scholar has written two books about her without her permission or approval.

When it comes to writing iwi history, however, or the life of a Maori person, especially a person seen as rangatira, it would be unthinkable not to have iwi, hapu or whanau permission to proceed. This is because within Te Ao Maori, those things – lives and histories – are seen as being corporately owned. Hence I would have received no cooperation from Tainui when I wrote about Te Puea Herangi, or from Moriori when I wrote about their iwi, had I not had formal and explicit permission to do so.

Does such permission imply other obligations? It can and it does, and I'll address that aspect of the topic later if there is time for me to do so.

Finally, should Maori history be a domain for solely Maori writers? My answer to that would ideally so, but not necessarily so. The much more important factor is that Maori history should be the domain of those who have equipped themselves to write it: who have the language skills, the cultural understandings, and the historical skills. Those people may be Maori; but not necessarily or inevitably so. I have to say that recent Maori history written by Anne Salmond, Angela Ballara and Judith Binney has been written to the highest possible standards, Maori or Pakeha. And that has occurred because those people equipped themselves to operate within Te Ao Maori with the admiration and respect of their peers, Maori and Pakeha. That's not to say that some of those peers wouldn't question their judgements or conclusions – because history will always be what it has been up to this point: an argument without end. But what one wouldn't question is their integrity and their competence, which in this context have nothing to do with their own ethnicity.

5.

Palimpsests and Imponderables?

A talk given as part of a panel discussion on historical writing (with Thomas Keneally and C. K. Stead), Christchurch Writers Festival, 2002

I have to say that my first reaction to the topic, and to the composition of this panel, is one that proves the validity of Robert Ardrey's territorial imperative thesis: novelists should butt out of history and leave it to the safer hands of historians.

I recall only too clearly the despair with which local historians and biographers observed Janet Frame writing her autobiography, in three volumes over four years, and in each of the years in which the volumes were published, winning the now extinct New Zealand Book Award for Non-Fiction.

How dare she? Wasn't she content with cleaning up the fiction award each time she published a novel? And why on earth should she win a *non*-fiction award simply because her books were well written? Well written, but careless of those features so beloved of professional historians and biographers – accuracy, names, dates, chronology.

That was my first reaction. My second was to remind myself about how *badly written* so many works of history are; and how many professional historians, obsessed with the very methodological features I've identified, professionalise themselves out of an audience because they give no thought to how to engage and hold an audience beyond their immediate peers: other historians.

In other words there are insufficient historians who give attention to being at the same time writers, to being literate, in the way Frank Sargeson used that term – not meaning 'able to read'; but able to write and read intelligently and aesthetically, giving attention to the shape and the sound of prose, to elegance, euphony and clarity, and to the work of one's writer predecessors in the form of echo and allusion. This absence is odd, given that our literature comes out of a heritage that includes such names as Gibbon, Macaulay and Trevelyan; and even more odd, given that our local pathfinders were such men as Reeves, Sinclair and Oliver – all three men poets in addition to being historians.

I have to say that in my own historical and biographical work, the 'literary' considerations are always given the same attention as the historiographical or methodological ones. And this is not for the purpose of pretension, or of showing off, or of building baroque prose structures (how does the expression go? 'If it ain't baroque, don't fix it'). It is for the purpose of making the reading of historical writing accessible, illuminating and above all enjoyable.

Having said that, I have to confess to being uncomfortable and sometimes displeased at the way in which some writers of fiction use history. Historians, for example, seek to reconstruct the past according to its own patterns, not contemporary ones. They seek to contextualise human behaviour and to represent it and explain it in terms of what people knew and believed at the time. So that you don't, for example, blame a colonial administrator of the 1840s for knowing nothing about Gandhi, Martin Luther King or James Belich, any more than you blame an eighteenth-century Maori navigator for being ignorant of Galileo or Copernicus. And, of course, you avoid anachronism. You don't have characters saying things like, 'Well, Mother, I have to enlist for the Thirty Years War now, because it's only got another year to run.'

One of the worst examples of this kind of fiction is Witi Ihimaera's novel *The Matriarch*, in which the heroic characters are brimful of knowledge and attitudes that are simply not contemporaneous with their lives. This novel also falls over because the author credits other historical figures, Prime Minister Peter Fraser, for example, with characteristics and values that he not only did not have, but which he abhorred. And this failure is plain and simply one of the author doing insufficient research. The best that can be said about this novel is that it is the *longest* written thus far by a Maori writer.

Another one that comes to mind is Maurice Shadbolt's *Lovelock Version*, in which an idiotic, ignorant blimpish Lieutenant Colonel named Malone makes a hash of a New Zealand attempt to take and hold Chunuk Bair in the course of the Gallipoli campaign. Now there *was* a New Zealand Lieutenant Colonel at Gallipoli named Malone, and he *did* lead the charge to take Chunuk Bair on 8 August 1915. But he was absolutely nothing like Shadbolt's fictional Malone – indeed, as in the case of Ihimaera's depiction of Peter Fraser, the real Malone represented the antithesis of the fictional values attributed to him. How do we know this? Because Malone kept a diary, and the diary survived the war. My argument with Shadbolt over this issue, which became public in a series of letters in the *Listener*, was that if Shadbolt had read the diary (he hadn't), he would never have portrayed Malone in that manner. Had he nonetheless wanted to do so, then he should have changed the character's name. Shadbolt's response, in essence, was that the writer of fiction can do what he bloody well likes, that *that* is the nature of fiction. To which my response was and is: it's not the nature of *good* fiction. Good fiction is plausible and invites the willing suspension of disbelief; poor fiction, of that sort, only generates disbelief.

At this point I'd like to personalise this discussion by savage criticism of the works of other members of the panel. I'd like to – but I can't, because I have no grounds for doing so. The two Keneally works of historical non-fiction that I've read, *The Great Shame* and *American Scoundrel*, fulfil all the criteria I've mentioned for good history. They are the fruit of broad and deep research, and they are beautifully written. I encountered neither an historical nor a stylistic wrong note in either of them, nor in any of Tom's historical novels.

I haven't read *The Singing Whakapapa*, which is, I suppose, the book of Karl's most relevant to this discussion. But I've read others with historical content – *Talking About O'Dwyer*, *Sister Hollywood*, *All Visitors Ashore* – and, again, found no fault with the history – or none I can remember. And they were unsurpassedly well written.

And so, on that note of unctuous benignity, I'll stop. Karl and I were placed on this panel on the condition that we took out a good behaviour bond and said only nice things about each other. I've said nice things about him – and I now vacate the rostrum in order to let him say nice things about me.

6.

Back to Shul

2002

Borough Park, Brooklyn, is part of New York City and part of twenty-first century AD American life. But the section of it that I visited on that Shabbos morning was so different in character from Manhattan that it might well have been another planet. The neighbourhood is made up of decaying tenements and shops dating from the late nineteenth century. Many of the shop fronts and businesses are identified in Hebrew lettering. The day I was there, being the Sabbath, the shop windows and entrances were sealed with aluminium doors.

What the stranger finds most striking, however, is the character of the inhabitants. The slightly shabby streets were populated by knots of men and boys, most speaking Yiddish, and most wearing long black coats and Homburg hats, or black caftans, round fur-trimmed hats and prayer shawls on the shoulders. The men were almost all beaded. Some displayed payos or uncut locks of hair falling in front of the ears. A few wore phylacteries on their foreheads. In costume and appearance, there was little to distinguish these groups from the inhabitants of shtetls in the eighteenth or nineteenth centuries.

The shul I was looking for was one of dozens of synagogues in this part of New York. There was nothing to reveal its identity on the outside of the building, which in any case was covered in scaffolding. One entered through a dark wood-panelled corridor that eventually opened out into what looked and smelled like an ancient school classroom. Part of the congregation sat facing one another on either side of a long bench. Most were either reading scripture or praying privately but aloud. Some were involved in intense discussion with their neighbours opposite. In the far corner a cantor was leading the singing and chanting in Hebrew and the congregation joined in sporadically. Those who appeared to be the most ardent worshippers stood at the front of the room, bowing rapidly or swaying as they sang and prayed. They were all men. Women were either absent or worshipping unseen in another part of the building.

Out in the corridor two congregation members were arguing loudly and coarsely in English and sounded as if they were on the verge of fisticuffs. Nobody inside took any notice. Neither those who were praying, those who were singing nor those who were involved in Talmudic dispute were distracted by the self-contained activities of others. And periodically everybody stopped what they were doing and joined in singing what seemed to be choruses, in high tremulous voices. The total effect was of a kind of orchestrated chaos.

I understood neither the forms nor the content of these complementary forms of worship and reflection. And I did not seek out anybody to interpret for me precisely what was going on, for two reasons. One was that I did not want to impede or interrupt the participation of any member of the congregation. The other was that I had not gone there in an analytical or anthropological frame of mind. I simply wanted to see, hear and experience forms of ritual that would have been part of my great-uncle's shtetl upbringing. And that unmediated, unexplained experience was eerily resonant.

When I closed my eyes and concentrated on the singing and the niggunim, wordless melodies, I could have been listening to Bedouin worshipping under the stars three thousand years ago. It was an ancient sound, redolent of an umbilical pull of continuity that linked these men and boys to their ancestors and to a powerful sense of identity and security. I was reminded of something I had read the week before in the Holocaust Museum in Washington, words of Rabbi Leo Baek preaching in Berlin on the Day of Atonement that followed the horrors of Kristallnacht: '[We] will turn our eyes to the days of old. From generation to generation God redeemed our fathers, and he will redeem us and our children in days to come.' There were no compromises made in this room in favour of comprehension, relevance or changing vernacular. This was ritual staunchly and proudly *unchanging*, 'from generation to generation'. It made the concessions to modernism of my own religion seem cowardly and symptomatic of a lack of confidence and conviction.

The other contrast with a more controlled and linear form of Christian service was in the fact that almost all the participants seemed comfortably at home in the midst of a diversity of activities – from grey-bearded men with thick European accents and prayer shawls now draped over their heads, to pre-adolescent boys with bright eyes and shiny cheeks, subject to grandfatherly attentions from the men and periodically bowing or swaying with as much energy as their elders.

The exceptions were a small group of men in adolescence and young adulthood who, after a time, began to eye me with undisguised hostility. I was sitting in a corner, formally dressed in suit and tie and David

Belgray's yarmulke. But my lack of active participation revealed me as an outsider. Their hostility turned to alarm when I reached into my jacket pocket, drew out a pad and pen and began to take notes. One of the young men got to his feet and disappeared. Seconds later a middle-aged man approached and leaned down to speak confidentially to me. 'You are welcome here,' he said. 'You are free to sit and observe or to participate. But you must respect our customs. And one of our customs is that it is not permitted to write on the Shabbos.' Of course. I should have deduced that. I apologised and put the pen and paper away. The young men continued to stare at me with displeasure.

Then, one at a time, half a dozen other men of about my own age came and sat with me for five or ten minutes and talked. They asked why I was there, and their inquiries were genuinely curious and not at all unfriendly. It was as if they were compensating for the flurry of disturbance caused by my blunder. I told them about my great-uncle, and about my efforts to find out more about his family and his geographical and cultural background. They displayed unfeigned interest in this quest and spoke of their own families' origins in Eastern Europe, some of them in Galicia, and of their own efforts to trace their antecedents back to specific shtetls.

The difference between their experience and that of the New Zealand Belgraves, they stressed, was that their families had chosen to remain loyal to their heritage and they took pride in the fact that a large part of the Jewish culture that had existed in pre-1930s Europe had been transplanted successfully in the United States. One, Bernie, made the point that, for him, the very fact of the Shoah created an obligation to preserve in America precisely what had been lost in Europe. That, he believed, was the meaning or the message of that unprecedented trauma. Like most people in the shul, he too had lost relatives by execution in the Second World War or in the Nazi death camps. Here in Brooklyn, he said, he brought up his children to know and understand the old religious laws and practices, using Hebrew for worship and scriptural reading and Yiddish at home. They went to Jewish schools. His wife worked for the family's income, but he did not. He followed the tradition of the Talmudic scholar and studied scripture and the commentaries on scripture and ensured that his family said the right prayers at the right time and observed the laws. They kept a kosher household and did not have television nor non-Jewish newspapers. In this way, he said, they retained their Jewish identity despite the temptations and abominations of the most materialist and most secular society in the world. That society lay 'out there', he said, just beyond the cultural frontier with which they insulated their way of life. And, despite its temptations, the United States had given him and his family sanctuary in the pre-war years when no other country in the world, including Palestine, would have done so.

All this was communicated to me in a friendly manner, without any hint of proselytising or criticism of my Christian heritage. But then I was joined by Judah, a heavily bearded man in his fifties, who took the seat opposite mine, fixed me with a baleful look and began what felt like an interrogation. Who was I? What was I doing there? By whose authority had I entered the shul? In contrast to my previous conversations, his was full of suspicion. To my shame, I decided to tease him, curious about what that might bring to the surface.

'Have you sought advice from a rabbi about what you are doing?'

'Yes,' I said. 'She encouraged me.'

Judah glared at me, palpably appalled. 'A woman? A woman can't be a rabbi. That is an affront to the law of God.'

'But she's Jewish,' I said. 'And she has a congregation, a religiously observant Jewish congregation.'

'She's not truly Jewish,' said Judah. 'Like all religions we have our apostates and heretics. Just because they *call* themselves Jews doesn't make them so. The difference between Judaism and other religions is that ours is commanded by God Himself and every action we take is in the service of God. The consequences for denying his will, therefore, are far more serious.'

Then he changed tack. 'Do you hope to *become* Jewish? Is that really why you're here?'

'No,' I said. 'I'm not Jewish, I can't be Jewish and I don't want to be Jewish. I have a religion of my own with sufficient strengths, weaknesses, oddities and prejudices to absorb a lifetime of exploration and reflection. But there is much I admire about the Jewish heritage and about Jewish thought. And, of course, it is ancestral to my own heritage.'

'It's not possible to admire Judaism *and* Christianity,' he said. 'They are mutually exclusive.'

'For you, perhaps, but not necessarily for me.'

'For God,' he said.

'That's fundamentalist,' I replied.

'God is fundamentalist,' he shot back.

'How do you know that?'

'From my reading of the Torah and the Talmud.'

I tried another change of direction.

'I admire the fact that people here worship and behave in a manner that goes right back to shtetl culture and beyond. But consider what riches flowed into European and human culture as a whole when the Jews began to leave the shtetls and the ghettos and to contribute to mainstream society. Lewis Namier likened the Jews of Eastern Europe to a glacier, part of which remained frozen up to the 1930s, other parts of which had melted under the rays of the Enlightenment and released a flow of marvellous talent. Where would the modern world be without the contributions of Freud, Einstein, Heinrich Heine, Moses Mendelssohn, Felix Mendelssohn? Where would Western civilisation be now if those minds and those talents had remained locked away in Jewish communities studying only the Talmud?'

'Ah!' said Judah. 'Now we're approaching the truth. If they had remained where God placed them, carrying out His wishes and commands, then what you call "civilisation", human civilisation, might well have been weaker. But God's civilisation, His plan for the redemption of the world, would have been stronger. There would have been more righteous men in the world, and the world might have been spared the Shoah.'

I paused before I responded to this, wanting to be very sure that I understood him.

'Are you saying,' I asked, 'that the death of six million Jews in Europe, and millions of gypsies, homosexuals and communists, was a visitation of the wrath of God because some of His people were not carrying out His will?'

'I'm saying,' he reiterated slowly, 'that that is a possibility. And it is a possibility which every God-fearing man ought to consider.'

'That,' I said, 'is as brutal and as wrong-headed as saying that the suffering of the Jews has been caused by their racial guilt for the death of Christ. What you have been implying,' I went on, 'is right. There is a gulf between our respective positions that no amount of words or arguments can bridge.'

'Then you have no right to be here if you are not willing to be led to the discovery of God's will,' he said. 'What you're doing amounts to nothing more than an act of cultural tourism.'

I couldn't wholly disagree with that. But the atmosphere between us and around us had become unpleasant. Other men had circled round us to listen in silence. I did not feel I had any right to take the moral high ground in a place that was neither culturally or spiritually my own. Nor did I know what histories or experience had imprinted on Judah the opinions he now held so passionately. So I got to my feet to leave. He looked disappointed. 'I hope I haven't offended you,' he said.

'No, I'm not offended,' I said. And I wasn't. I was uncomfortable. And I was made more uncomfortable by the fact that one of the reasons I wanted to escape was to write down the very discussion we had just had, before recollection of it dimmed.

'Shalom,' he said, and shook hands. I made my way out on to the street to look for some kind of coffee shop where I could sit, have a drink and write my notes. But my search was fruitless. All eating and drinking places were closed for the Sabbath. So I did the job perched on a fire hydrant and attracted odd looks from passers-by. Then, I realised, my wanderings had disoriented me. I approached a group of behatted and prayer-shawled young men heading to or from the shul of their choice.

'Do you know where the nearest subway station is?' I asked one of them.

He stopped walking and looked uncomfortable. 'Yes, I know where it is,' he said after a long hesitation. 'But I can't tell you.'

'You can't *tell* me?' I was perplexed. Then, of course, I understood. 'You mean you can't tell me for religious reasons?'

'Yes,' said, looking relieved that I had said it. 'I'm not permitted to tell you.'

I wandered off looking for a Gentile or a liberal Jew or even a non-observant one. Could this have been the kind of thing that irked my great-uncle? Would he have become impatient with the kind of God who required people to wear fur hats and black clothes at the height of a New York summer, and *not* to direct strangers to the subway on a Saturday? I didn't know. I would probably never know. But the idea took hold of me in the form of an unexpected insight: it would have been just as possible to feel smothered by the blanket of Orthodox Jewish culture as it would have been to be comforted by it.

7.

What I Believe

1993

The marvel of consciousness – that sudden window swinging open on a sunlit landscape amidst the night of non-being.

Vladimir Nabokov

Theologians used to tell those of us who were listening that one of the faculties that distinguished our miserable species from the beasts was the power of reflection: not only to know, but to *know* that we know. And that this power in turn generated anxieties that have persisted from the time of the earliest recorded ideas – and far beyond that too, from the vaults of ancestral thought, silent to us now because we have no evidence of the voices that once filled them. Who are we? Where do we come from? Where are we going? What is our relationship to one another? How ought we to behave?

Because I am a historian, not a theologian, I don't believe that there are 'right' or 'wrong' answers to these questions. Just answers. And the answers differ because those who ask them filter the replies through different preoccupations; and because the contexts and evidence available to the questioners change from culture to culture and age to age. My responses, for example, are conditioned by the fact that I was born in mid-twentieth-century New Zealand of Pakeha antecedents, raised a member of the Catholic Church and educated in Western traditions of thought. Had I been born in Peking or Baghdad – or in fifteenth-century Aotearoa – then I would have evolved a rather different view of my place in the cosmos; but one that would be no less valid for the time and place in which I grew to consciousness.

Another consequence of my being an historian is that I can best make sense of the principles and opinions which guide my behaviour by tracking their origins and growth. They did not strike in a bolt of lightning on the road to Damascus; they were not siphoned from a single repository of wisdom. They developed as a consequence of a particular sensibility coming into contact with a range of experience and ideas. 'In my end is my beginning . . .'

My earliest memories are of growing up on the Pauatahanui arm of Porirua Harbour in the early 1950s. I would wake in the morning with the windows open and my first experience of each day was the smell of flowers and fruit, or of rain on earth, that came to me from the garden into which my bedroom projected. Frequently I got up before dawn to fish, making my way through the macrocarpas and pines to the beach. I wrote about this in *Being Pakeha*. It is a sequence I have only to close my eyes to recall in sentient detail:

> I would collect the oars, rowlocks and fishing gear from the shed, then walk the short distance across sand and shell to the water's edge. By this time the sun would be lighting the crests of hills around the harbour, and they seemed to hang in the sharp air. The boat would be anchored knee deep, in still water reflecting the surroundings as faithfully as a mirror . . . I loved the dip of the oars, the creak of rowlocks and whisper of water along the sides of the boat. The sun would be coming up over Pauatahanui as I slipped past the bleached shellbank we called cockleshell island. In the channel where the water ran green and deep, opposite Moorhouse Point, I tossed the anchor over the bow and paused until it gripped. Then I baited the rod with mullet, released the line into the deep, and waited with exquisite anticipation . . .

This experience, along with the weekend excursions into bush below the Paekakariki Hill, or walking around the rocks from Titahi Bay to Kaumanga, or Hongoeka to Pukerua Bay, contributed to what I would now recognise as my earliest spiritual feelings: a knowledge that I was part of nature and nature was part of me. I felt at home in a boat on the water, trees were companionable presences, the cry of the oyster catcher was the last comforting sound I heard at night as I fell asleep.

Parallel with the unconscious development of that cosmology was the growth of another, which did not touch me anywhere near as intimately. At the Plimmerton convent school we were drilled daily in catechism by nuns of the order known colloquially as Blue St Josephs. 'Who made you?' 'God made me.' 'Who is God?' 'God is our Father in Heaven.' 'Why did God make you?' 'God made me to know, love and serve Him in this world, and to be happy with Him forever in the next.' It was a rote-learned formula, like the eight-times table, designed to make us loyal and conforming members of a two-thousand-year-old institution.

By the time I was eight I was deemed to have reached the 'age of reason'. This meant I had assimilated – and could regurgitate at will –

sufficient catechism to be prepared for my First Communion. I now knew that God had created angels to share with Him the joys of Heaven; that some of those angels had rebelled with Lucifer, who became Satan, thus initiating the age-old struggle between Good and Evil.

God had made the earth in seven days and placed Adam and Eve there. They, tempted by Satan, had eaten from the forbidden fruit of the Tree of Knowledge. This was the Fall and it resulted in their being driven from Eden, and in all their descendants being stained with Original Sin. From that time on humankind suffered pain and death, the earth became a 'vale of tears'. The descendants of Adam and Eve were unable to qualify for entry into Heaven. Christ, however, Son of God, became man and suffered and died to redeem us from sin. From henceforth Heaven was open to those who accepted God's grace and lived in it.

Each night I made an obeisance to this order of things and launched my petitions to the benevolent Deity: 'Dear God, please bless Mummy and Daddy, Louise and Terry, Nannie, Gran and Jimmy, and all my relatives and friends. And let Granddad rest in peace. And please God make me a good boy. Amen.'

These two cosmologies – one based on nature, the other on religious instruction – intersected when we went to Sunday Mass at Pauatahanui. I described this in *Being Pakeha*.

> On those charmed days we drove around the harbour early in the morning, the water as flat as sheet-steel. We looked for herons and for the ripples of mullet trying to outrun kahawai and kingfish. The church itself, built in local wood in 1878, stood alongside cabbage trees, kowhais and macrocarpas on a hillside above Stace's Flat. In spring and summer the sacristy doors were thrown open and we could see grass and trees outside behind the altar. Families who had built the church – the Abbotts and the Murphys – had their own pews. The

> windows were papered with peeling pictures of Christ and assorted saints. The wood of the walls and pews was stained dark with varnish and age . . . In later years I could never smell incense or burning candles without that simple, solid building and its occupants coming forcefully to mind.

After Mass we stood outside in the sun, swapped news of family comings and goings with other parishioners, and heard about the seasonal vicissitudes of farming. All the while the birds sang around us and sheep grazed safely on the flat below.

As I grew towards adolescence, the Catholic Church and its traditions imprinted on me gifts more enduring than the theology of the catechism. The ethics of Christianity, communicated through instruction in scripture, stories of the lives of saints and – most especially – through the living examples of my mother and Catholic grandmother, shaped my character and my view of the way I believed people ought to behave towards one another.

I was fortunate to escape the spirit of Jansenism that pervaded other pockets of Catholicism in New Zealand. The Christianity I grew with was of a largely cheerful and positive kind, a religion that stressed the redeeming power of love rather than mortification of the flesh and punishment for a range of trivial sins. 'For God did not send His Son into the world to condemn the world, but so that the world might be saved through Him.' And it would be saved through love: love of God for humanity and of humanity for God and for one another.

The practical application of this formula stressed to me most often was the one of doing unto others as you would have them do unto you. I was taught too that the most profound satisfaction came from service, from giving rather than taking. In the lives of the nuns who taught me I saw daily evidence that this was so.

> Where there is hatred, let me sow love; where there is injury, pardon; where there is doubt, faith; where there is despair, hope; where there is darkness, light; where there is sadness, joy . . . For it is in giving that we receive . . .

At home and at school I was heavily imbued with the message of the parable of the talents. Each individual was born with an obligation to change the world for the better, and of those to whom much was given, much was expected. After despair, the greatest sin was that of refusing to recognise, to develop and to use God-given gifts. In addition to being a prescription for spiritual growth, this was also the basis for an activist and optimistic approach to worldly problems.

Out of these beliefs developed a conscience, a loud and active instrument that regulated my behaviour. It served also to keep me honest. In the religious atmosphere of my childhood there was no ambiguity or hair-splitting about the nature of truth. Truth was, in the Thomistic phrase, the agreement of the mind with reality. Disagreement of the mind with reality – self-deception or telling lies – was a sin against both God and nature and troubled me greatly. It also made life more complicated ('Oh what a tangled web we weave . . .'). I came to place a high value on honesty, not simply as a moral imperative but as a condition necessary for peace of mind.

Catholicism's other enduring gift was an awareness of the power of language and ritual. The Latin Mass was a source of profound solemnity and joy. There were the embroidered vestments, the mannered movements, the mysterious manipulation of bread and wine, the consecration bells. At High Masses there was the addition of incense, chanting and singing. But, above all and at all Masses, there were the words. In the beginning indeed was the word . . .

The effect began with the sound of the Latin, sonorous, oratorical and highly pleasing:

Credo in unum Deum,
Patrem omnipotentem,
factorum caeli et terrae,
visibilium omnium et invisibilium.

Added to this, the meaning of the words filtered through to us through a slightly archaic Biblical idiom which intensified the gravity and the beauty:

I will wash my hands among the innocent
and will encompass Thine altar, O Lord,
that I may hear the voice of praise
and tell of all Thy wondrous works.
I have loved, O Lord, the beauty of Thy house
and the place where Thy glory dwelleth.
Take not away my soul with the wicked
nor my life with men of blood
in whose hands are iniquities
their right hand is filled with gifts.
But as for me, I have walked in innocence.
Redeem me and have mercy on me.

We basked in the knowledge that these words and the movements and gestures that accompanied them constituted a ritual hallowed by time and history. They had been practised unchanged for centuries. Our forefathers in England and Ireland had risked death to hear these radiant and sacred sounds. And this very same liturgy was being celebrated in precisely the same way, minute by minute, in almost every other country in the world. It was an umbilical cord that bound us to the past and penetrated national cultures. It was, we believed, unchanging and unchangeable.

It was also, I realised later, subversive. The capacity to be able to respond from an early age to the impact and resonance of words was to make me susceptible to other words, other messages, other values. As I began in early adolescence a great odyssey through English, European and American books, I encountered the power of words shaped by other men and women. There was beauty, wisdom and terror in all literature, and much of it addressed the kinds of questions that I had thought were the sole preserve of religion. The psalmist had asked God, 'What is man that Thou art mindful of him?' But Lear on the heath asked 'Who is it can tell me what I am?' And even Foreskin, to bring the process up to our own place and time, asks more laconically – as becomes a New Zealand male – 'Whaddarya?'

Such cries arise from the deepest recesses of the human psyche. And, along with tentative, matching answers, they pervade the literature of all cultures – reminding us, if reminding we need, that in matters of the mind and spirit, all men and all women of all ages are contemporaries of one another.

How much of the experience and knowledge there is of life, and of death, in Shakespeare. Who can fail to be affected by the profundity of such lines as, 'Man must endure his going hence, even as his coming hither. Ripeness is all.' These flashes of understanding that extend human consciousness out into the void recur in Dante and Goethe, in Eliot and Yeats, in Sargeson and Baxter. They illuminate the ignorance and darkness that surround us, they feed me and sustain me. 'Teach us to care and not to care, teach us to sit still.'

I am not suggesting that Catholics alone have the capacity to respond to such a message. But I do believe that those who grew up conditioned by a liturgy that recognised the power of sound and graceful metaphor are more susceptible to such a response. And it is that reality, not conspiracy, that lies behind the accusation that there has been a Catholic Mafia at work in the world of New Zealand letters.

The liturgy and surrounding culture of my childhood accustomed me also to regarding music as a form of spiritual expression and healing ('You, alone . . . say an existence is wrong,' says Auden of music, 'and . . . are unable to pour out your forgiveness like a wine'). There were, of course, the songs of the Mass and the Benediction service, all redolent of sanctity and solemnity. But I was saturated too in those marvellous Latin hymns which embellished the liturgy proper: Cesar Franck's 'Panis Angelicus', Gounod's 'Ave Maria'. In addition to listening to them in church, I heard them at home, sung by my mother and grandmother, a consequence of their time at Porirua after the First World War when their family had made up the entire parish choir with a repertoire as large as that of any city church.

The effect of this background was to make me as interested in and appreciative of music as I became of literature, to be as much moved by aural harmony as by the judicious arrangement of word, thought and feeling. I experience in Handel's 'Largo' a microcosm of beauty, sweetness and pain encountered in a lifetime; and in Camille Saint-Saëns' 'Organ Symphony' a magnificent assertion of the human spirit in the face of disappointment, death and corruption ('And death shall have no dominion . . .'). It is through these media – words and music – that humankind does achieve a degree of immortality; or, at least, the ability to send messages of wisdom and hope from generation to generation.

Something else happening throughout my childhood and adolescence was to leave an imprint on me. Growing up at Paremata, I was surrounded by the evidence of one thousand years of human occupation: remnants of moa hunter camp sites in the dunes; traces of pa and middens around the harbour; whale ribs and vertebrae in the vicinity of what had been Thom's whaling station; and the remains of Fort Paremata, erected at the harbour mouth in 1846 to intimidate Ngati Toa. These relics gave me a strong sense that the past was close to and connected to the present, the two dimensions rubbing against each other to produce a frisson that animated everything that one saw and felt in such a place. And this in turn merged with my love of books to produce a passionate interest in history that would in time become a professional occupation.

> In James Cowan's *The New Zealand Wars* I found a detailed description of what had happened militarily in the neighbourhood . . . It was supplemented with maps, photographs and descriptions of combat that enabled me to pinpoint and stand on each site; and once standing there, to imagine that I was experiencing what had happened there . . . These experiences made history live for me. I felt the presence of people who had gone before. I saw them in a kind of Arthurian world that was not in Camelot but, literally, on my own doorstep.

Once I had become professionally involved in the study of history it had other consequences that contributed to my values and views of life. The major one was a feeling of benevolence in the face of human diversity, inconsistency and fallibility. If indeed the 'proper study of mankind is man,' then such a study reveals a catalogue of expectations unfulfilled, of acts and expressions of moral fervour that turn out to be disguised self-interest, of movements of millenarian promise that lead, inevitably, to disappointment. The effect of such a study is an acute awareness of how high human aspirations can ascend and how far, like Icarus, they can fall. One develops an immense tolerance for the infinite human capacity for failure; but also a respect for the fact that, in the face of eternal disappointment, individual after individual and generation after generation is prepared to raise high the banner of hope and march towards some notion of a better world. 'How brave, how bright with beauty, man's brief and bitter day.'

There is the fact too that historians tend not to be as judgemental as other people about the past, because they recognise that the past can only be understood in and on its own terms. People are always limited by the viewpoints of their age, and by the amount of information and the degree of insight that has reached them. It is as foolish to castigate a Pakeha colonial in New Zealand of the 1840s for lacking the perceptions of a Gandhi or Martin Luther King – or a James Belich – as it is to blame a sixteenth-century Polynesian navigator for his ignorance of Copernicus and Galileo. People can only be judged in terms of what they knew and felt, of the options actually open to them – not on the basis of the information available to the contemporary scholar.

The study of history has bequeathed me another conviction, one that is sharply at variance with the manner in which my early education – particularly my religious education – was carried out. It is the belief that truth must be sought through the media of unfettered investigation and open disputation according to the model of the Open Society as characterised by Karl Popper among others:

> a society whose members may openly criticise the institutions and the structures of power without fear of reprisal; where education is distinct from indoctrination; where freedoms of thought, action and belief are allowed the greatest possible extent . . .

My commitment to this process has its basis in positive and negative factors. Negatively, I cannot but be aware of the harm caused in the past when cultures and regimes have attempted to impose orthodoxies by dictum or by force. Tyranny over the mind is as iniquitous and ultimately as productive of discontent and violence as tyranny that seeks to control movement and behaviour.

Positively, however, I believe that freedom to think and to draw conclusions according to evidence is simply the most efficient and the most efficacious way to discover and test one's own truths. Jack

Shallcrass described well what is at stake in a talk to the student congress at Curious Cove in the mid-1960s:

> If we treasure the right to be heard, then we must accord that right to every other person. If it is correct for us to deny any person or any section of the community any right, then by change of circumstances he would by correct in denying us . . . Freedom for the expression of someone's wrong idea secures freedom for the expression of my right idea. Error is essential to the finding of truth. What we know depends equally on knowing what is and is not the case. Hence the futility of enforced orthodoxy – for we can only know if its view is right if we also know other views.

What, then, am I left with as a consequence of the intellectual and moral journey I have outlined? My views on the value of literature and music, on the lessons of history, and on the role of the Open Society – all these remain much as I have described them.

I also retain a large part of the code of ethics that came to me from my Catholic upbringing, particularly the emphasis on honesty and service. I reject the prudishness about sex and eroticism that was part of that code, however (though the uncommitted promiscuity of the '60s and early '70s was equally fallacious); and I reject the intellectual totalitarianism that characterised our religious education.

I no longer believe that an Intelligent Being orchestrates the workings of the universe, nor that He intervenes to correct our follies. I no longer believe because these propositions are contrary to logic and to the evidence of my mind and senses. This realisation that nobody is 'in charge', however, far from invalidating the code in which I was brought up, makes its practice all the more imperative. Because if we don't regulate our lives and our behaviour towards one another, there is nobody else to do it other than the State; and that alternative, while unavoidable on occasion, is scarcely preferable.

I retain too the sense I originally derived from religion, reinforced by a study of history, that we are not flies of a summer living in a continuous present. We are products of our past, and we are linked to continuities that come to us from our histories. I believe too that people who live without visible reminders and reinforcements of that connection will be prone to anxiety and disorientation.

I no longer believe that human life is eternal in the sense that we maintain our individual consciousness after death. I have encountered no evidence to support such a belief, nor would I wish for such a reprieve – would a spouse derive any consolation from watching the partner or the children he predeceased grow old, decay and die?

As I have indicated already, however, I do believe in the power of literature and the arts to convey thought, feeling, even wisdom, from one generation to another. It is in this sense only that individuals achieve a degree of 'immortality'; and in the way in which they influence the lives of those with whom they come into contact, especially their descendants.

I no longer believe in the existence of Good or Evil as entities separate from human existence. But I believe strongly that good or evil impulses reverberate beyond the individual lives that initiate and experience them. 'The evil that men do lives after them . . .' So does the good. And I consider myself, in part, an amalgam and a continuation of the inspirational examples I have been set by a succession of mentors, some of whom I knew (my mother, Ngoi Pewhairangi, Ormond Wilson), many of whom I encounter through the miracle of literature.

Scriptural references to eternal life – 'Eye has not seen, nor ear heard, nor has it entered into the hearts of man the things that God has prepared for them that love Him' – are no more and no less than poetic statements of the spiritual rewards to be gained from leading a good life. The fruits of those rewards, the peace and satisfaction of mind and spirit that they may bring to us and those associated with us, constitute the Kingdom of God; and they are experienced by us only in the course of the single life we each receive.

I believe that we do indeed possess 'spiritual' faculties; but that these are the most complex form of the consciousness that in some degree pervades all living things. As conscious flecks of matter we come from dust – or, in the metaphor of another culture, from Papatuanuku; we shed brief light into the darkness around us; then we return to dust. That dust has the power to give and sustain life again, but not in a form that we shall experience.

There is for me mystery in this process, something awesome and something holy. It presents the spectacle of life continually renewing itself, of matter demonstrating its recreativity. And this is another sense in which life can be considered eternal, and in which the traditional language of religion continues to have meaning. If we revere life, then life itself may prove to be eternal; if we don't, it won't.

Recently I returned to live on the shore of a rural estuary. My motives for doing so are complex. Such a location enables my wife and me to replenish ourselves in a more direct relationship with the natural world – the sea and its creatures, the bush and birdlife, the unspoiled landscape. But there is more than this going on. I am also returning to the shapes encoded on my psyche in childhood when I grew up alongside identical land forms and seascapes. And, when I look down the estuary, between the hills to the ocean beyond, I see more than a view that is beautiful and invigorating in its constantly changing aspects of light and colour.

I see also the elements capable of sustaining the gift of life. And, in the coming and going of the tides, in the rise of mist and the fall of rain, I see a reflection of the deepest mystery and pattern in all life: that of arrival and departure, of death and regeneration.

It is in this process that I apprehend what I would now call God. Not the image of our childhood: the old man with a long beard in the sky who intervened in human affairs when necessary – literally a deus ex machina – to unleash floods, deliver tablets of stone or deposit his son. That was a metaphor that sought to make sense of the complexities of the human psyche. The God I experience is infused in the regenerative power of the natural world, in its balance and its gravitation towards wholeness. In the words of Bishop John Shelby Spong:

> The healing powers of the human body and the regenerative power within the natural order to adapt and to overcome enormous abuse for me point to the . . . presence of the creating God. Creation itself demonstrates an unquestioning ability to adjust to new circumstances while continuing its own inner destiny to achieve a purpose and a fullness that I can only glimpse. To me, these are the natural footprints of God . . .

This is close, I suppose, to a Gaian view of the earth and every creature on it making up a single organism. Such a metaphor is in harmony with the way I experience creation and our relation to it and to one another. And it serves to emphasise the corollary to this view, the dark shadow that it casts over the future of our planet and our species: just as the earth has the power to spawn and sustain life, humankind now has the capacity to interrupt that process, to inflict death without regeneration, departure without arrival. In our ability to strip the earth of its resources, to perforate the ozone layer, to trap industrial gases within the atmosphere, above all in our ability to unleash the destructive power of a thousand suns, we not only have the means to exterminate our species. We now have the power to kill God.

I have no strong inclination to close on an apocalyptic note, simply to be realistic. What preserves me from despair at the prospect of humanity's infinite propensity for greed and annihilation is the matching power and pervasiveness of that force which we share for life and for altruism, and to which I attach the name of God. 'And for all this, nature is never spent,' writes Hopkins. 'There lives the dearest freshness deep down things; And, though the last lights off the black West went, Oh, morning, at the brown brink eastward, springs . . .'

And I pray that it will ever be so. For the gift of life, in the tolerable circumstances in which my compatriots live, is precious and enriching. Without being sure precisely to whom I owe gratitude, I am thankful that I share it.

8.

Jerusalem 25 October 1972

1977

It is 2 a.m. We see the lights of Jerusalem unexpectedly after thirty-two miles of winding darkness from the turn off. The massive dining hall on the marae glares into the night. The tent in front glows like a lantern. People are moving back and forth between them. Here, suddenly, there is life. And death. Jim Baxter lies in an open coffin inside the tent surrounded by his family and commune.

The body has arrived only an hour ahead of us (there was red tape in Auckland and trouble on the road). The first mourners are still going into the tent, shoeless and on their knees, to see Jim and to console the living. We join them and wait for the slow procession to shuffle forward.

I am here because I have to be. To repay a private debt. To farewell a friend. To say goodbye for two others who can't come. And to verify that he is dead. I had read about it the night before in a Wellington dairy and couldn't believe it. I had always imagined him growing old. At home I dug out my first letter from him. I was further shaken to find it dated October 22, 1965 – seven years to the day before he died.

I was surprised I had known him that long. The letter, in the cramped biro writing that always seemed an incongruous vehicle for eloquence, was attached to some notes on writing that included the advice: 'The fact that you live in a community of cripples doesn't mean you are obliged to be a cripple.' It was a reminder to be true to myself and a rationalisation for nonconformity. Maybe that was why I was confused about the length of our relationship. The Jim Baxter who lived out this nonconformity so completely was a far more recent person than the postman poet who sent me the first letters.

I couldn't find any other correspondence then. Only the little crucifix he once left behind like a seed, and a slightly crumpled piece of paper on my office wall. I put both into my breast pocket. As I kneel at the tent flap I feel them to reassure myself that this man did indeed drift in and out of my life for seven years; to confirm a reality that has become blurred with the news of death, the quickly stifled grief and the exhaustion of the long drive.

The person in the coffin is certainly dead. He is not the man I first knew – the postman with the long lugubrious face and the strands of hair that fell diagonally across his forehead; the sportscoat with disproportionately large shoulders, the baggy grey trousers and leather shoes. This man is the friend of Hamilton and later Wellington days. He is bearded and patriarchal. He looks priestly and, for the first time I can remember, handsome and relaxed. His hair and beard are trimmed. His face is made up lightly, as if for a television appearance. A triumph of the mortician's art. He displays a physical dignity in death that was purely spiritual in life. He needs no consolation.

The people around him do. They are clinging to one another and crying. As the boy in front of me moves I face a girl I have never seen before. She is very young with blonde hair. Her eyes are red-rimmed. Before I begin to move towards her she is already reaching for me. We hug each other around the neck and she shakes and sobs. She holds me more tightly. After a few minutes the pressure releases slowly and I kiss her cheek and move on. I repeat the embrace with men and women around the tent until, in spite of being tired and drained of feeling when I arrived, I begin to absorb their grief and cry with them. I pass two children asleep under blankets and a dog lying between them. I see John Baxter silent but attentive. I see Hilary. The water in her eyes seems deeper than that in any others and doesn't flow. She hangs on, almost desperately. Next to her, her mother, the widow. Jacquie is slumped against the displaced coffin lid beside her husband, her eyes closed. She lifts her head, looks at me hard and accepts the greeting without recognition or response. She slumps again like a glove puppet without a hand.

I move slowly round the coffin looking at Jim and remembering how much he approved of the tangi as a way of releasing emotion and sending off the dead. I see the familiar blotches like calamine lotion above the eyes – not disfigurements, but emblems of humanity and mortality. I talk to him quietly. I thank him for good advice and for accepting me without reservation and tell him my problem is fixed. I tell him Phyl and Chris want to be here but can't come – one stranded by distance, the other anchored by recent illness. I tell him they love him as he loved them. I compliment him on being a superb craftsman and the shrewdest publicist I ever met. He listens passively and accepts what I say. I resist an impulse to touch his forehead with my hand. I know he will be cold.

On the other side, more mourners. Greg Whakataka grasps me and whispers 'Kia ora, brother'. I whisper back 'Kia kaha'. He pushes me back slowly, and smiles. Then draws me to him again and we hongi. Wehe the kuia, Jim's old ally, sits by the tent flap. I hold her right hand in both of mine and we press noses for a long time. She begins to tangi. Tears run down her cheeks and make my lips wet when I kiss her.

I stand up again. My knees are stiff and sore. Outside the tent in the harsh light again, Ray and I walk the few yards to the dining room. I am cold and saturated with sorrow. Three couples huddle together on the steps, not seeing us. We shake hands with two men at the door. Inside, Rowley invites us to have some food from one of the three long trestle tables. I'm not hungry, but I accept the cup of tea one of the women from the pa pours me. People are moving in and out with sleeping bags and blankets. Some are sitting at the tables. Others on forms around the walls. Selwyn Muru is interviewing Toro Potini, who is saying complimentary things about 'Mr Baxter' into the microphone of a portable tape recorder.

I sit down next to a writer, a near-contemporary of Jim's. Maurice Shadbolt has known all the phases of Baxter's adult life except one, the last. We talk and fill in gaps for each other – he tracing the years back from the postman, I bringing them forward from the Burns Fellowship. We talk wearily but compulsively, trying to make sense, looking for the reassurance that comes from seeing connections and patterns in our lives.

He tells me that in Auckland the previous week Jim began to look up people he had scarcely seen for years, including Shadbolt. He tells me how, earlier that month, unprompted, he had begun rereading Baxter. He describes how Jim died in a stranger's house on the way back to Jean Tuwhare's after his first medical examination in years. He speaks of something strange that happened outside Taumarunui as Jim's family brought the body back to Jerusalem.

I tell him more about Boyle Crescent, about Jerusalem, about the first squatting in Wellington, and about the itinerant Baxter, padding round the country; a Socrates parents feared would seduce their children

– not because he coveted their property or their prestige, but because he didn't. And because he attracted young people who didn't want to inherit sterile rituals and values. We talk about his personae of alcoholic, persecuted public servant, postman, writer and Christ. I suggest it doesn't matter what kind of role a person assumes. What matters is how that role shapes a person's behaviour and how it activates the people with whom he comes into contact. The people Jim Baxter wanted and needed to know in the last years were the alienated young. And they are the ones most obviously here tonight, many of them now able to talk and relate to other people as a result of having known him. They are the ones who call him Hemi rather than Jim, who view him as saint rather than poet. Shadbolt seems to be stranded beyond them at some more distant high-water mark, although he understands. He knew Jim's compassion and is not surprised about where it led him in the end. The ethical pulse, he says, was strong in him from the beginning.

I walk back to the tent where these people are keeping Jim warm with a quilt and with company. Taura Eruera of Nga Tamatoa is standing in a far corner talking to him. He farewells him with the solemnity of an old kaumatua. With his Afro hair and grey blanket he looks like the subject of an Angus portrait. He stops intoning. The people in the tent, lying down, sitting or kneeling, watch him and listen to his silence too. They are waiting for something. It happens. Taura speaks again, this time in English, and tells them what he said. He formally acknowledged achievements, Jim's understanding of Maori things and his communication of these things to others. He farewelled him as he went to the spirits of his ancestors.

Now, without telling others what to say, he tells them how to say it. And shows them. He compares the tangi to the two faces of a coin. The one commemorates a man's death, the other celebrates his life. 'Just stand up when you have something to say and say it. Don't be frightened of pauses.'

No one analyses what is happening or imposes any kind of shape on what follows. It just grows. A poroporoaki. A litany of tributes, testimonials of lives changed, stories, tears, laughter and songs. There is the priest Father Theodore who says he learned more about compassion hearing Jim Baxter's confession than he did in seven years in the seminary. There is Johnny the former nightclub singer who found an identity at Jerusalem with Jim Baxter after travelling halfway round the world. He sings the Lord's Prayer in a powerful but cracking voice. There is Greg who says Jim led him back to God and clasps his Bible as he speaks. He has established his own commune. And Milton who says that Jim reprimanded him gently for not knowing his own language and that he has begun to learn. He plays the guitar and repeats a few words in Maori over and over again. Wehe hangs on to the coffin and chides him: 'Oh you, you old fighter. You've gone and left me to fight alone.'

A theme emerges slowly, in fragments. Jim Baxter pushed up a yoke that people hung on to. The disciples now feel they must support others in turn. When the talk slides towards mawkishness and tears, somebody reminds us that Jim wouldn't approve. He'd sit up and fart and shoot another angel. Or somebody tells a story like the time he compared intercourse with contraceptives to an orange without pips, but admitted it still made good marmalade. Hana Jackson turns her sorrow towards the bereaved and then bursts into song: 'He's got the whole world in his hands.' Tame Iti does 'Tutira mai nga iwi tatou tatou e' and a haka. Always, we talk to Jim as much as to the others and look at him as we stand up one by one.

I try to convey my awe at the number of lives this man touched, shown in the number of people here I have never seen before. I talk about his insight, his care, his teaching by example and analogy. I take from my pocket the piece of paper and read what he typed for me (after I complained about his writing), St Francis' Canticle of the Sun that he like to recite in the sun. At the end:

Be praised, oh my Lord, for our Sister Bodily Death
From whom no living man can escape—
Woe to those who die outside Your friendship,
Blessed are those whom death discovers at rest in Your holy will
For the second death shall not harm them.

No, it shall not. And no one here is afraid of death just now.

Nobody reads his poetry or talks about poems. He was a man who established his reputation firstly as a poet and who will be remembered for literary accomplishment. But the people here are not scholars and critics. They are talking to a friend, a brother, a father, a social worker, a constructive shit-stirrer – not to a literary figure. They are talking to the man who had relationships, not the man who wrote about them. The literati will come tomorrow for the burial, perhaps. Or make their evaluations in learned periodicals. Tonight is the harvesting of the last three years of his labouring in non-poetic fields.

At dawn I leave the tent and walk through the wet grass in the middle of the old marae to watch the sky lighten and Jerusalem become visible. The tightness in me when I arrived has gone. The silhouette of the church on top of the hill whitens. The dark hills over the river become green. The negatives become positive.

Birds are starting to sing, but they are not native birds – no tuis, bellbirds or fantails to be heard, only thrushes and blackbirds and sparrows. The hill in front of me rises out of the dimness into a settlement: church, tombstones, convent, Victorian houses, willows, pines and apple trees – a piece of European landscape transplanted here for the security of Pakeha pioneers remote from their origins. But behind me is the old meeting house, dark and full of ghosts. The boys are already bringing wood down the hill for the hangi. The people who live here, who filled these buildings before the commune came, are Maori. And the ritual working itself out here is a tangi.

Back at the tent I collect my friend. We have to return to Wellington and work four hours away. And we want to be out before the crowd arrives and it becomes difficult to identify the people as individuals. We shake hands, kiss and hug. One long, last look at Jim, at rest with his friends. Then a hongi and another kiss for Wehe. She hums in her throat as we hold each other. I give her a koha to help with hospitality. 'Come back soon,' she says. 'You know where we are.' Yes, I know.

We drive out of Jerusalem along the river road. On the hills high above us ponga, cabbage trees, totara and rimu are regenerating. Their thin lines advance from the ridges down towards the settlement where Jim Baxter's bones will become part of the earth.

9.

Tangata Whenua: Origins and Conclusions

1977

I suppose I am the survivor of a dying breed: the sympathetic Pakeha journalist who for a time specialised in writing about Maori things in the footsteps of Rusdens, Cowans and Ramsdens. I propose extinction of the species because such a job almost always leads to well-intentioned idealisation; and because eventually there will be sufficient Maori writers with surer insights than I into the workings of two cultures. Yet I haven't apologised for my work. Interest and personal growth are one justification. The aspirations and wishes of my informants are another. I have helped also to make Maori preoccupations more intelligible to some non-Maori New Zealanders. Frequent encounters with ignorance and prejudice in European circles reminds me that the process is far from complete. (I am not suggesting here there is no 'ignorance and prejudice' in Maori opinion – only that I feel my influence limited to the formation of Pakeha attitudes.)

The most recent example was a community leader (a former service chief of staff and National Party candidate) who told me that Maori who demonstrated grief publicly during mourning ceremonies for Norman Kirk were 'a clamorous minority trying to advertise themselves for dubious ends'. Further, harmonious race relations in New Zealand 'depend on an acceptance that Polynesians are destined to be hewers of wood, drawers of water and bulldozer drivers. That's where their attitudes lie, that's the kind of work that brings them satisfaction. Those who tell them otherwise create expectations that can't be fulfilled and lead to agitation.' All this from a man who seeks and may yet hold further public office.

Yes. Such conversations reinforce the view that the process of communication between Maori and Pakeha is barely established. There is still a need to put people like this in touch with others of differing background whom they would be unlikely to meet because of social or racial insulation; with John Rangihau of Tuhoe, for example, whose avalanche of words from dozens of conversations and interviews swamps me still with eloquence and common sense:

> I am always surprised by the number of Pakeha people who know better than I do how I should be a Maori and what is good for me as a Maori. I would never be so audacious to suggest to Pakeha how to live as Pakeha. Yet I am continually being told that to be a New Zealander I must accept absorption of many Maori things into European culture. I can't go along with this because I don't feel I can be some sort of Pakeha. What's more, I don't *want* to be Pakeha. There are a lot of things in the Pakeha world I do not like as against those in the Maori world that I do. But I have been asked by the majority culture to become a Pakeha to a large extent so that I can stand up and be counted as

> a New Zealander. Cor blimey, I *am* a New Zealander, a Maori New Zealander, and you can't take that away from me.

This passage speaks much to me about the failure of communication and the persistence of patronising public policies. Both, to a large extent, are results of a reluctance on the part of journalists to pursue preoccupations unfamiliar to them.

The *Tangata Whenua* television series was the most ambitious and painful project that has tried to redress an imbalance in the media. Since its completion, I have felt an impulse to set down some things we encountered. I followed this impulse eventually because I believe our experience illuminates corners of New Zealand life not often open to public view; and because it sets out some cautionary tales for journalists who follow me in such activities (and in spite of my wish they be Maori, subsequent experience has shown they are not likely to be).

First, the question why the series was made is not rhetorical. It cropped up in a multitude of places and situations. 'What right have you people got to be here? What are you taking from us?' The answer for me was not simple, even if it had to appear so to satisfy an impatient local obstructing a camera lens.

Tangata Whenua had its origin in my experience as a newspaper journalist and author. I found myself often in emotionally-charged situations. But I found it difficult to represent these situations (karanga, tangi, oratory, singing, argument) in words alone. So I became aware that film was potentially the most arresting, affecting and practical way of transporting other people to them. That there was some value in so doing I have never doubted. People who don't participate in the cultural options available to them neither know nor grow in their own country.

Then, as a television critic, I began to chastise the NZBC for not making use of this vastness of unexploited material. A Maori audience had a right to see its own values and rituals reflected on television sets for which they had paid licence fees. Further, the experiences to which I was referring were far more dramatic in film terms than the stream of action songs that purported to represent the 'other' New Zealand.

After two years of chipping away and then talking to NZBC staff, I realised that the propositions I was suggesting were the kind everybody agrees with because the ideas were worthy; and because agreement is the quickest way to get rid of an irritant. But immediate commitments of broadcasting officers and an absence of spectacular evidence from me resulted in continuing inertia on the part of policy and programme makers. People like Bill Kerekere and Selwyn Muru were interested. But their hands were tied in Maori ways and their shoulders bowed under existing responsibilities. These last factors were important. Because when people said to me later 'Why you?' – as if I had just bowled on to the scene – I could say and *had* to say: 'Because you wouldn't or couldn't.'

So. I crossed the gap from critic to film maker. I discussed an idea for a single programme with a very helpful Michael Scott-Smith and presented it as a general script to John O'Shea and Barry Barclay of Pacific Films. We made one documentary on contract for NZBC and it became the first in a series. The impact of the participants, Barclay's skill in converting ideas into cinematic images and O'Shea's persuasiveness in the rarified atmosphere of NZBC decision-making produced a series commissioned in 1973.

Part of the answer to 'why *Tangata Whenua*?' is that I wanted to, I promoted an idea, and (as part of a production team) I swayed the NZBC to the conviction that it was a good idea. The other part is that after more than a year of discussion, the people who were to emerge as major participants in the series thought it was a good idea too and wanted to be part of the project (I'm referring to John Rangihau, Ngoi Pewhairangi, Piri Poutapu, Herepo Rongo, Dick Stirling, and so on).

It was this later part of the production process – the conversations with communities and eventual filming – that threw up the incidents and conclusions I think worth sharing. I offer them in the form of warnings and positive advice to those who follow us, and as idle entertainment for the idle.

What follows is selections from a journal in which I noted down our progress under loose subject headings. (Begun because Barry Barclay said at the beginning: 'You realise the NZBC will want us to make some sort of report on this.' Understandably, the NZBC didn't. It was too introverted by its own dismemberment to care about the clangers we dropped and the precedents we established.)

Pace

We have discarded all concepts like time and relevance. It's partly because of a rural mode of communication, partly a Maori one. There is a strong suspicion and dislike of the city hustler who breezes in with preconceived ideas and tries to mould people. The tempo that works is a bit like the one you adopt for a tolls operator: 'transfer charge, person to person, number calling, person calling, number charged to, number calling from, who's calling' – if you break the sequence or accelerate the pace you destroy the rhythm and communication collapses. Within the right tempo, you have to approach the subject of conversation in slow concentric circles, deal with it, and back out gradually the way you came in.

Interrogative interviewing too is out for old people. You have to nominate the subject and then let the interviewee talk without interruption, whaikorero-style. It's slow but it's worth it. Given time to think at their own pace, people are more likely to come up with verbal gems. Or, if you want short answers, set up a group conversation making clear what you want. If it is not clear, be reconciled to a little shooting and a lot of editing.

Cultural Differences

The Chilean cabernet disappeared in a matter of seconds. Te Hiti said, right at the beginning of the party: 'Save yous fullas beer. Don't waste it on us. We'll get rid of the plonk first.' (No suggestion of political boycotts at Ruatahuna).

The groaning table (euphemistically called a 'cup of tea' but embracing sponges, trifles, fruit salad and cream) has to be dealt with, in spite of work or diets. It is the ceremonial way of removing tapu from visitors. Eating with people, especially those who don't speak English easily, is a major way of cementing relationships. It gives hosts confidence and makes them far happier about discussing more consequential things, later.

Living communally requires total dedication. It's not easy if you're not used to it: at Tokomaru Bay, if you escape from the marae for a walk along the beach and some precious moments in your own company, one of the locals will spot you, catch you, apologise for neglect and think of things for you to do – like taking you back to the kitchen or down to the pub. If you are 'of the people' you have to be 'with the people', very much in the plural and very often.

Breakfast fishheads are to be chewed. The juice is sucked out, the unswallowables spat on to the plate. Eyes can be eaten separately. Brains are said to be small, but worth it if you can find them. Ted suggests 'pollution (rotten corn) and rice bubbles' as a truly New Zealand breakfast for the Hotel Intercontinental menu.

The Arikinui's council questioned me closely on the programme proposals. I had explained it all in my written submissions to them weeks earlier. But they hadn't read them. Koro tells me 'he kanohi kitea' – a face seen is an argument understood.

The crew, unwillingly, are learning the conventions: don't touch an old person's head or pass things over it (they will tolerate these things, coming from ignorant Pakeha, but not make much effort to cooperate); don't sit on a food table; don't wash your hands in the dishes' sink; don't talk about tapu things over food or cigarettes; stand to reply to a welcome and, if it's inside a meeting house, don't move about while you talk; give a donation when leaving; sing when asked to, especially if the host has sung first; avoid beginning new projects on a Friday. Little things. But, cumulatively, they add up to acceptance or rejection.

Maori Language

It would be impossible to do this kind of work adequately without some knowledge of spoken Maori: to introduce yourself in acceptable, comprehensible terms; to reply appropriately to formal welcomes; to explain your purpose fully; and (in some key cases) to interview non-English speakers. More than any other factor it has been the one that has made the difference between a positive and negative community response to our overtures. It's also seen as a symptom of sincerity of interest. Doors have been closed in the past because of a literal lack of understanding about people's purpose, or assumed lack of caring deduced from ignorance of basic Maori. ('How can they expect us to believe that they really want to record something of our Maoritanga when they don't even care enough to learn the language,' says Eva. 'Would they send a camera crew to France without someone who could speak French?' The answer, of course, is Yes. At least they've sent people off to Asia, New Guinea and the Islands this way.)

Incongruities

Moses Wharepouri assures me there's no prejudice at Parihaka. 'Everybody's welcome here,' he says. 'Everybody. Chinks, niggers, wogs, the lot.'

Communication Problems

Barry, wanting to get out shooting again before dark, causes consternation in the hotel dining room by calling across the floor to the manager: 'Have you got something hot that comes quickly?'

Soundman Craig asked the old folk for one minute's silence for the atmosphere track on his tape. Thirty seconds into it, mokoed Te One Whero asks: 'Should we close our eyes and bow our heads too?'

The 'selected community spokesman' was a disaster. He seemed ignorant, nervous, inarticulate. His wife kept butting in impatiently, prompting him. In the end we filmed the wife instead, to everybody's consternation.

Unexpected Hold-ups

After briefing and setting up we are all ready to roll. There's about half an hour's daylight left. Then Whitiora begins his mihi (formal welcome). Then a series of prayers. Then a hymn. 'Now we can start,' he says brightly. It is dark. We'll have to shoot the interview tomorrow.

After half a day of discussion and explanation we are ready to film the burial with the consent of everybody present (some 300 people). Then a carload of relatives who haven't heard of us arrives and wants to know just what the hell we think we're doing. Fair enough. By the time we finish telling them, we've all missed the ceremony.

At Granny Moetu's tangi it takes all night to debate whether we can film. They are also arguing over who should keep the tribal relics for which the deceased was caretaker. Some of the old folk confuse the issues and think I want the relics too. The argument is intense.

Hoani hasn't been able to drink for several days because of the ritual. Now he's thirsty. And he thinks, incorrectly, that beer makes him talk better. Each time we change location and set up he polishes off a bottle.

I've decided to do the remaining interviews in one place, so they retain some coherence.

Unexpected Hold-ons

After the wrap at the golf course we sit down to morning tea with the talent. Then Herepo gets up and begins to call – to everything: us, the meeting house, her ancestors, the lot. Keith was up and filming again and Craig recording in less than a minute. It proves a point: it's no good the crew complaining they haven't got as much time to set up as they got with instant-pudding commercials. The best things in life and film just aren't arranged that way.

We waited two days to interview Dave. He kept disappearing or making excuses or feeding us. He wasn't ready. Then, as we were packing at 6 a.m. for the early flight to Wellington, he rang: 'When are you fullas coming over? I've been waiting all night.' We do a full day's shooting.

Spooks and Nightmares

Peter woke up screaming again tonight. Swears he saw another face at the window. Eva assures him it's only her great-great-grandmother keeping an eye on us. I suspect a cow, until I go outside and see his window is twelve feet from the ground.

As we set foot on the Wainui Marae in moonlight, a dog begins baying up the valley. The mournful sound is taken up by a few others, one at a time. We decide to wait in the car with the headlights on.

Unexpected Happenings

Yesterday Te Kani warned the farmer and his neighbour not to stand under the pohutukawa where they used to dry out the bones. Someone would drown, he said. Somebody always did if people stood under the tree when he lived there. The two culprits laughed and stayed. Today we keep getting interrupted by an Orion aircraft looking for the bodies of a man and his son who had been lost fishing off the coast.

When we finished the Te Kooti interviews, the light stands toppled and crashed. The ground was even and there was no wind. John says there is a price to pay for this kind of thing. We're lucky it's only lights.

As we left the cemetery a child dashed across the main road and was hit by a car. He's in Rawene Hospital. Some of the old people think it's us. We've caused an aitua. Meretiana has had a bad back continuously since it happened.

Today a fire broke out after we'd finished shooting at Takapuwahia. It just went woof in the long grass next to the marae, like spontaneous combustion. It's the second time. The same thing happened at Raglan, where we had to beat the fire with wet sacks. This time, the Porirua Fire Brigade puts it out.

Over-organisation

This weekend we shot in Hamilton for the opening of the Maori language seminar, at Panmure for the opening of the Tuhoe meeting house, at Herne Bay with the Stirlings for the leadership programme, back to Hamilton for a teaching session, back to the Stirlings in Queen Street, and then to the Ringatu services at Panmure. And Ngoi is hurt because we don't think highly enough of her to film the hui at Tokomaru Bay.

Tangata Whenua is over. The films may be screened again on television and they are being shown in schools. But the filming has finished. And I never want to be associated with a process like it again. I never again want to interfere so directly in the intimacy of people's lives, nor play God by advising what bits of them should be represented and what shouldn't.

But I'm glad we did it. First, because we established precedents that should open the door to continuous Maori programme making: we showed Maori situations to be informative and entertaining; at best, they can be as emotionally charged as anything seen on television; thanks to voiceover translation, Maori language need not be a barrier to communication with a mass audience. Secondly, the series initiated community television of a kind – the participants rather than the film makers chose the outlines and emphases of programmes, a precedent for more interesting television and for a more diverse representation of community feeling and opinion. Thirdly, reviews like this of Harry Dansey's, in the *Auckland Star*, were enough to extinguish most of my flickering doubts:

> For this emotive and disturbing weekend *Tangata Whenua* was the guide I needed to point me to the fact that present tensions are transitory, and we all in the end, like Herepo's twelve children, will lie quietly beneath a pine tree or, like her ancestors, uneasily under a golf course. I have no idea what effect the efforts of Michael King and Barry Barclay had on others. All I know is that last night when I needed it, they showed me the soil from which I sprang and the past that explains at least in part the emotions of the present.

Thank you, Harry. The final thing I learned, I think humbly, was that writers need feedback if they are to develop. And some of that feedback has to be supportive to confirm the impulse to move on to the next project.

10.

Approaching a Distant Peak: A Biographer Discovers Frank Sargeson

2003

My childhood, spent in and around Wellington, differed from those of most of my contemporaries in perhaps only one important respect: I knew that there were writers in New Zealand; and I knew that it was possible to *be* a writer in New Zealand. Hence becoming a writer always seemed to me to be an achievable and unsurprising ambition. I knew these things because we had a house full of books, many of them written by New Zealanders, and because we knew some of the people who wrote some of those books.

My father, obliged to leave school at the age of twelve to help support his family through the Great Depression, had done what a significant number of gifted and creative New Zealanders did in the 1930s and

1940s: he joined the fledgling advertising industry. There he met and worked with such artists as Mervyn Taylor, Russell Clark and Eric Lee-Johnson. He interacted and socialised with writer-journalists such as Pat Lawlor, O. N. Gillespie and Eric Ramsden. And, after he took Denis Glover into what was then the agency Carlton Carruthers du Chateau and King, he joined Denis for Friday night drinking sessions at the Royal Hotel in Lambton Quay, with Jim Baxter, Lou Johnson and Anton Vogt. Maurice Duggan too joined Carlton Carruthers in Auckland, but the year after my father left, as did Christine Cole in Wellington.

The writers who actually visited us most frequently in the 1950s were Glover, Lawlor, detective novelist Elizabeth Messenger (who had married one of my father's friends from adolescence), and, a little later in the decade, M. K. Joseph. Glover, after provoking several incidents of raucous disorder, was eventually barred from the house because my mother disapproved of the fact that he was not married to his partner Khura Skelton – and, to tease her, he boasted of the fact. Pat Lawlor, however, a Catholic gentleman, displayed none of the wild and anarchic qualities associated with some members of the writers' tribe, though we did discover later that he had been, like Glover, an alcoholic. And Pat took a special interest in me from his family bach at Plimmerton because I, like him, had a bout of childhood polio. Unlike him, I recovered without a limp.

Now Pat Lawlor – poet, novelist and non-fiction author, historian of early twentieth-century Wellington – was *not* a great New Zealand writer. At this distance most of his work, especially his imaginative writing, seems mediocre. But he was warm and generous towards those who were interested in writers and writing; and he was in every sense of the word a 'bookman'. He sold books by mail order. He collected books and book plates. He gathered and regaled stories about writers. He reviewed books prolifically. He founded the writers' organisation PEN in New Zealand. He was the first secretary of the Literary Fund

Advisory Committee. And he introduced me to Frank Sargeson – not in person, but via Sargeson's books.

One of the things Pat liked to do over a long period of time was to rate New Zealand writers – the way a racing form guide would rate horses and their chances. Katherine Mansfield held place of honour in his pantheon; Eileen Duggan was close by. Jim Baxter's position tended to move up and down, depending on his recent behaviour. Sargeson's position was also variable and dependent on Pat's moral view of the writer's most recently published characters and plots. He was most ill at ease – I realised later – in the company of any text which had about it what he regarded as an 'odour' of deviant behaviour.

It was Pat who first showed me the unpretentious pamphlet-like edition of *Conversation With My Uncle and other sketches*, the Progressive Publishing Society's plain edition of *A Man and His Wife*, the John Lehmann London edition of *That Summer and Other Stories* with its jarringly inappropriate English seaside town cover, and the slightly later Lehmann edition of *I Saw in My Dream*, whose jacket (as somebody remarked) looked like an advertisement for the purity of New Zealand butter. Pat clearly disliked what he assumed to be the nature of Sargeson's sexual morality (and, it occurs to me now, he probably knew of Sargeson's conviction for indecent assault in Wellington in 1929, though he never dropped a hint about this to me). But he was nonetheless impressed by the undeniable fact of 'London publication' and 'overseas reputation'. And, I heard him say more than once, it was possible that Sargeson would inherit the Mansfield mantle, if only he could be persuaded to lift his gaze from the sewer.

While Pat lent me some books, Sargeson's were not among them. He was hypersensitive to any suggestion of 'corrupting' the young (he knew and liked to quote the passage from St Matthew's gospel about millstones being hung around the necks of those who did so). He probably believed, as did many at the time, including Michael Joseph, that homosexuality was potentially contagious and disposed its victims towards paedophilia. I had instead to seek out Sargeson's volumes in the library of my secondary boarding school. And I sought them out with all the more relish because of Pat's hints about dark doings. I was then disappointed in them: first, because the 'immorality' was oblique and difficult to locate and understand; and secondly because of what seemed to be the inordinately limited viewpoint and vocabulary of Sargeson's characters in the stories of the '30s and the '40s. I was far more taken at this time by the lush textures of Evelyn Waugh's *Brideshead Revisited* and *Sword of Honour* trilogy. Sargeson's prose by comparison seemed so sparse as to be almost barren.

And yet seeing those books of Pat's had an effect, as did his toying with the notion that Sargeson might be on the verge of greatness. And that effect was reinforced by the opinion of an English teacher whom I respected that Sargeson was a writer deserving of an international reputation. I became conscious of Sargeson, not as somebody one was likely to spot on Lambton Quay like Baxter or Glover or Vogt; or, even, encounter among the parties of the Wellington literati; but, like Glover's friend the fabled Fairburn, a kind of lofty peak just visible in the far distance, like Tapuaenuku on the Kaikouras, spotted ghostlike from the Wellington coast on exceptionally clear days.

Much later, in adulthood, other stories – some heard, some read – attached themselves to those first impressions. How Sargeson 'saved' Janet Frame by taking her in when she made her escape from psychiatric hospitals. How he had been a mentor figure to a wide range of other writers, including the so-called 'Sons of Sargeson'. How he lived monk-like in a fibrolite bach on the North Shore and shared his food and wine, his company and his conversation, with a wide range of friends, some of them not in the least literary.

Then there were the later books – *Memoirs of a Peon*, *Joy of the Worm* – which I eventually read with far more relish than the early ones. I was especially interested in the fact that much of the latter novel arose from the history of the marvellously clever and marvellously batty Cook family, who had been closely involved with the life of Oakley Sargeson, Frank's uncle. And Oakley had died when my friend Nigel Cook was working on his King Country farm in 1948. Reflecting the length of their family association with Frank, Nigel and his older brother Bert referred to him as Norris, his given name.

I was to learn far more about Sargeson, however, as a result of teaching journalism at the Wellington Polytechnic from 1971 to 1974. My boss there was Christine Cole, former wife of the writer and Sargeson protégé John Reece Cole. Chris, a writer of considerable flair in her own right and soon to be a publisher too, had known Sargeson for a quarter of a century. As a result of John Reece Cole's descent into illness and mania, Chris had replaced him as Sargeson's executor and beneficiary. Some of their lively correspondence of those years concerned arrangements for the disposal of Frank's property and modest income. But much of it was wicked lively gossip about the world of writers and writing. Chris passed these letters on to me for my delectation; and she spoke of Frank always with concern, admiration and love. I began to sense that he provoked not simply respect and piety among those who knew him well, but something far stronger, something unprecedented in New Zealand letters.

This was also the period in which *Once is Enough*, the first of Sargeson's three volumes of autobiography, appeared. This title and those of its sequels – *More than Enough* and *Never Enough* – were suggestive of Nellie Melba's series of 'positively last appearances'. But they revealed a man at the height of his verbal powers in his eighth decade and they were books with which I could identify wholeheartedly. They engaged as narrative; and they were at the same time insightful reflections about the business of being human, and in particular about being human in New Zealand. By means of pointed storytelling and analysis, by a judicious mixing of documentary truth, fable and metaphor, they contrasted the Old World cultural inheritance of Europe with what had been transplanted and nurtured in the New World. At one level they were a justification for a life lived as an artist in New Zealand at a time when New Zealand was not especially welcoming of such figures. At another they were a marvellously evocative account of the variety and the sheer interest of human character, motivation and behaviour.

Throughout these years Chris said two things to me like recurrent mantras: 'You *must* meet Frank, you'd so enjoy him'; and, 'Of course age is taking a toll on him, he's well past his best.' I would have liked to have met him, the proverbial legend in his own lifetime; and to have walked through the hole in the hedge on Esmonde Road, Takapuna, and drunk Lemora in the house through which every New Zealand writer of note seemed to have passed over the previous forty years ('[Your] book makes clear,' Karl Stead had written of *Memoirs of a Peon*, 'Why coming through your hedge to take my share/I have to bow low'). I too would have liked to 'bow low' and 'take my share'. But what possible interest or advantage could there be for Sargeson in such an encounter, especially if his health was uncertain and social engagements increasingly tiresome for him? Besides which, I still lived in Wellington and visited Auckland only infrequently.

Oddly, it was my first trip to Europe that gave me what I felt was a valid reason and an opportunity to visit Sargeson. In 1976 I won the Katherine Mansfield Fellowship, which took me to Menton, France. From there I attended an international congress of PEN in London. And as part of the adventure, I found myself sitting next to a florid cherub of a man on a bus tour of 'literary London'. He introduced himself: he was John Lehmann, now approaching seventy and what would turn out to be the last decade of his life. I was overcome with awe at the prospect of keeping this Eton-educated protégé of Leonard and Virginia Woolf entertained for the full duration of an afternoon bus tour.

Unsurprisingly, Lehmann gave every appearance of being disappointed and profoundly bored having to sit next to an unknown writer from the Antipodes. He looked around somewhat desperately, hoping, I imagined, to catch the eye of Iris Murdoch, or Stephen Spender, or John Betjeman, who had also piled into the bus. Or anybody else. But without success. There was only one flash of animation in the course of the desultory conversation that followed. 'How's Frank Sargeson? Give me news of *him*.' To which I could only reply that I'd never met the man. Lehmann's eyes bulged in astonishment. 'But it's such a *small* country,' he said, 'with such a small population, and so few writers.' I concurred, and said that I did know people who knew him, and told him a few second-hand anecdotes. But the moment of interest had passed. 'Well, if you do meet him, say I asked after him,' said Lehmann. Then he appeared to fall asleep, just as we approached Charles Dickens's house in Doughty Street.

I came home early the following year via Auckland. I had lunch with Nigel Cook, who had moved north, and he said, 'Let's visit Frank.' I agreed, feeling that I had a pretext for doing so beyond simple curiosity. I was not disappointed. Despite being, supposedly, 'past his best', Sargeson seemed a good decade younger and considerably more animated than Lehmann, who had in fact been born four years after him. He was alert, attentive, almost fussily hospitable in his dispensing of rusks and Lemora. And he had especially penetrating eyes that gave you his whole attention. He was shorter than I expected and slightly stooped. This posture, the flashing of his eyes and the sharply pointed beard gave him a goatish appearance.

He laughed when I told him about the encounter with Lehmann, and he seemed pleased to be told that he was in better physical shape than his former editor and publisher. There were two major surprises in the conversation that followed, however. One was his voice, which was slightly nasal and very ordinarily 'New Zealand' in accent (I had expected something rather more like Maurice Duggan's fastidious and educated tone). The other was that he appeared genuinely interested in my opinions, and in Nigel's, and went to considerable lengths to draw us out. When he discovered that I was Catholic, he wanted to know immediately if I had done my 'Easter duty' and if not, why not. He said he always ensured that his friend Harry Doyle got to Mass at least once a year to fulfil that minimum religious obligation. He then spoke of what he regarded as the golden era of European civilisation, when a whole family of nations and cultures had been united by pre-Reformation Catholicism. When Nigel and I failed to take issue with this proclamation, he then did so himself, with reference to the fates of Copernicus and Galileo.

When it came time to leave, he began to fumble in his pocket for change. I couldn't believe it. Was he going to give us fifty cents to buy an ice cream? But no, he was offering us the bus fare back to the ferry which, he assumed, would take us back to town. He was surprised to learn that we had come by car, and that either of us could afford to own one – though Nigel's much abused Toyota was far from luxurious. Despite the volume and the noise of traffic over the hedge on Esmonde Road, he didn't regard cars as part of his world, nor of the world of the kinds of young people who would call in to visit him (this was not long after he had won the Katherine Mansfield Award for his story 'Just Trespassing Thanks', based on the behaviour of a group of bohemian youngsters who frequented Esmonde Road at that time).

The following year, still living in Wellington, I was commissioned to record a series of radio interviews for the Concert Programme called 'Looking Back'. I noted that March 1978 would be the month of Sargeson's seventy-fifth birthday and I asked producer David Delaney if he would send me to Auckland to interview the writer to mark that occasion. I stressed how seminal his influence had been on two generations of New Zealand writers. After checking with radio archives and finding that there was little there from or about Sargeson, Delaney agreed. He said that I should encourage Frank to talk about his life as a whole and what he felt it added up to.

To my surprise, Frank agreed to the proposal which, inevitably, would interrupt a substantial chunk of his working day (although, as I discovered later, that working day was now much truncated as a consequence of age and illness – he had only one more new book to come, *Tandem*, written in association with Edith Campion). I had no idea why he complied until I was writing his biography nearly twenty years later and read the correspondence for this period of his life.

It turned out that, like John A. Lee, Frank believed that he had been placed on a broadcasting blacklist, because of his criticisms of the declining standards of radio programmes and the appalling vulgarity of television. He also though that his falling-out with former *Listener* editor Monte Holcroft might have had something to do with his being banned from the airwaves. All this was a consequence of his love of conspiracy theories, his inability to believe that most events in life occur randomly, and the fact that he was most energised by a sense of persecution, even when no such persecution was occurring. He hadn't been asked to be on radio for many years: therefore he had been banned. QED. It was transparently obvious. The fact that I was coming to interview him meant that the ban had been lifted. He thought that Ian Cross, former *Listener* editor and by now chairman of the Broadcasting Council, might have had something to do with the rehabilitation. The scenario was abundantly clear to him. And it was nonsense. I had simply asked a producer if I could interview Sargeson and the producer had said yes.

On the day of the interview he greeted me so heartily that I wondered for a moment if he was drunk. He wasn't, but he was in a state of high excitement, something I later head Dennis McEldowney refer to as 'anticipation fever'. But, look here, he said, he had a suggestion to make. Why didn't we do the interview first without recording it, so that he could familiarise himself with the ground we were to cover and try out his answers. And then, suitably primed, we could do it again more confidently on tape. Foolishly, and because I wanted to maintain his spirit of exuberant goodwill, I agreed. We went through the interview the first time and he was voluble and sparkling. Then we did it a second time on tape and he became self-conscious, stiff, and, in comparison with the first performance, far more succinct.

He told me when we had finished that the double performance had been a test. He had made the same request to a journalist who had interviewed him some years previously, and the man had run the tape surreptitiously during the rehearsal. He had never spoken to that man again, he said. Nor would he have spoken to me again had I done the same. The whole episode was infused with the kind of Sargesonian paranoia that was a flip-side to his openness and generosity. But again, years later, when I was writing his biography, an alternative explanation occurred to me. I was coming to interview him about his life. I was coming from Wellington, the scene of his court case and shame fifty years previously. I had told him that Pat Lawlor was a family friend. Pat almost certainly knew about Sargeson's conviction for indecent assault. Did Frank imagine that I too knew and that I was going to spring a question on him about that episode in the course of the interview? Was anxiety about this possibility the reason for his almost manic gaiety at the time I arrived?

I'll never know. Because at that time I was wholly ignorant of that most traumatic event of his life, which had led to his abandoning Wellington, disqualifying himself from the legal profession and assuming a new name and new identity. And by the time I *did* know, Frank had been dead for a decade. Again, writing his biography in the 1990s gave me a new perspective on all this.

I discovered that the month before I interviewed him, Frank had been approached by Bert O'Keefe, one of his former colleagues in the Public Trust Office in Wellington, wanting to renew their friendship. Frank declined the offer, and he declined to invite O'Keefe to a celebration of his seventy-fifth birthday at Wheeler's Bookshop in Remuera. As I noted in the biography, the last thing he would have wanted was a tipsy O'Keefe blurting out secrets from their shared past, especially when he had managed to keep his Norris Davey life separate from his life as Frank Sargeson for nearly fifty years. But all this established that the issue of his conviction and its consequences would have been close to the surface of his mind at the time I arranged the interview.

Twelve years on, when I began to write the Sargeson biography, there were questions that I wished I had asked Frank on that day in March 1978. Not every biographer gets the opportunity to interview his subject, especially when the project turns out to be a posthumous one. But at that time, fresh from the publication of my book on Te Puea Herangi, hooked into a further study of Maori history that was to persist for almost another decade, I had no idea that I would become Sargeson's biographer. And even if I had known that, I would not have trespassed into territory that Sargeson himself was unwilling to disclose. 'To the dead one owes the truth,' Voltaire had written, 'and to the living one owes respect.'

The ground we did cover in the interview, however, represented the contours of his life that Sargeson *was* prepared to make visible in his lifetime. As to what happened beyond that lifetime, I don't imagine that he greatly cared, other than hoping that his writing might prove to be of enduring interest and importance to his compatriots. Thus far, that hope has not been misplaced.

11.

Yet Being Someone Other

2002

One of Laurens van der Post's best-known books bears the titles *Yet Being Someone Other* – a projection of his conviction that deep within himself there resided more than one person. It's a feeling with which I am all too familiar. I've often felt that the same phrase would make an apt title for a book about my own life; or, more specifically, about aspects of that life which arise from being moderately visible but living well short of celebrity status.

Those of us who inhabit such a dimly lit gallery are forever meeting people who think they ought to know us – from newspaper photographs or television – but who don't get their identifications quite right. My wife, for example, fell in love with me under the impression that I was the Ponsonby poet David Mitchell.

The problem first attached itself to me in the late 1970s, however. Then, for a time, I had a moustache but not the later fully fledged beard. I also wore, and still wear, spectacles. This Groucho Marx-like conjunction gave me a resemblance to another, better-known New Zealand writer.

I was made aware of this one morning on the footpath outside the Alexander Turnbull Library. A man with military bearing and a crisp English accent seized my hand and said he'd long wanted to meet me. I was, of course, gratified. Who, apart from Janet Frame, wouldn't be? He went on to say that I'd made a larger contribution to an understanding of New Zealand culture than any other single person. I was even more gratified, but recognised that this compliment was excessive. I imagined it was a prelude to being asked a favour. But no such request was made. Eventually I disengaged myself so as to (as I told my admirer) carry on my modest contribution to an understanding of my native land. As I left he said, 'It's been a real pleasure talking to you, Mr Shadbolt.'

So that was it! I was collecting compliments destined for a friend and colleague. Maurice Shadbolt was moderately pleased when I told him about the encounter, but not hugely enthusiastic about the fact that I'd been mistaken for him. He was even less pleased when I told him that if ever I was arrested for disorderly behaviour, for – for example – bathing naked in the Cuba Mall fountain, I would simply give the police his name instead of mine and no doubt all would be forgiven.

Six months later we were both in Bloomsbury, in a pub with the expatriate New Zealand writer Dan Davin. When Davin's friend Martha McCulloch came over to our table, gentlemen that we were, we stood to be introduced. 'This is the well-known New Zealand novelist Maurice Shadbolt,' Davin said, pointing to me. And then, indicating Maurice, 'And this is Michael King. I believe he writes history.' Maurice and I resumed our seats disconsolately and didn't say anything further at the time.

Now, more than two decades later, with more books than Shadbolt to my credit and features that look nothing like his, I might have expected this kind of problem to evaporate. It hasn't. A recent example:

At a function in Auckland celebrating publication of my Janet Frame biography, a Christchurch artist whom I admired but had never met walked over to me and began to abuse me for being a blinkered and fanatic nationalist. I listened politely, a fixed smile on my face, even though what he said did not seem to match up with anything I'd written. Two weeks later he wrote to me: 'I want to apologise for my unconscionable behaviour,' he said. 'I thought you were James Belich.'

Early this year I saw an elderly acquaintance who has associations with the early New Zealand film industry sitting alone at a café table in Whangamata. He had recently celebrated his ninetieth birthday. We hadn't seen each other for more than ten years. I joined him at his table and his face lit up with unfeigned delight. 'Peter,' he said, 'what a pleasure to see you. And congratulations on *The Lord of the Rings*. I hear it's doing very well.'

My heart, as they say, sank. Had I shaken off the persona of a prominent novelist only to be mistaken for a world-famous film director? Was the 'non' in 'non-fiction writer' shorthand for non-entity? Slowly, patiently, I went back to basics, reminding Brian who I was and how we had met. He was immensely apologetic. 'But you do look like him,' he affirmed, 'no doubt about that. And you are wearing shorts.' I was indeed. But never again . . .

Dennis McEldowney insists that I'm lucky. He's never been mistaken for anybody, he says, not even for himself. And I should also take consolation, perhaps, from the fact that some other writers are now being identified as me. In the course of leading a literary tour, I took my group to a central North Island café that is decorated with memorabilia from the New Zealand Wars.

'What are you doing here?' the proprietor's wife asked the man ahead of me in the tea and coffee queue. 'We're on a literary tour.' 'Oh,' she said, 'in that case you'll be interested to know that Marilyn Duckworth was here last week with the historian Michael King.' I leaned forward. 'Are you sure it was Michael King?' 'Oh yes,' she said, 'I recognised him from the pictures on the covers of his books.'

A subsequent check revealed that Marilyn had visited the café in question. But not with me. Her companion turned out to be Wellington writer Nelson Wattie – who is even now reeling from his own sense of unreality after a recent *Listener* bylined one of his reviews 'Nelson Wattle'.

There is another problem related to all this: that of having the same name as somebody else who is famous – or not famous, as the case may be. When Maori comedian Mike King won the Entertainer of the Year award, I received several congratulatory cards, One of these expressed additional admiration for the fact that I was Maori (I am not) and that I had not sought to take commercial advantage of the fact in my writing.

In our sesquicentennial year, I was lucky enough to be awarded a 1990 medal, for services to New Zealand literature. At least, I was told in a letter from the Minister of Internal Affairs that I was being offered such an award. But it never arrived. Months later, walking down Lambton Quay, I met an official from the minister's department. 'Congratulations on the medal,' he said. 'What medal?' I asked. 'I haven't seen it.' Puzzled, the man went back to his office to investigate. The medal had been sent to a Michael King, but not to me. The lucky recipient was an Air New Zealand reservations clerk who lived in Glenfield. He had expressed himself surprised but pleased by the award. Understandably, he was reluctant to give it up. He had been, as he said, a very good reservations clerk.

The only thing worse than cases of mistaken identity, perhaps, is the fear expressed by Ronald Hugh Morrieson: that he might become 'another one of those poor buggers who get discovered when they're dead'. But, no, there actually is something worse that that: the premature obituary.

This summer, after I had been interviewed on our beach for a documentary on recent New Zealand history, a bystander wandered over to me as the film crew packed up. 'That man talking to you,' he said. 'Didn't he used to be Austin Mitchell?' Used to be? 'He was Austin Mitchell,' I said. 'And he's still Austin Mitchell. He's just thirty years older than he was when he lived here.'

But it was too late. Notice had been given, with unmistakable clarity, of the next phase of my life. One day soon, as I hobble down our country road, grey-haired, grey-bearded, looking more like an Orthodox rabbi than Maurice Shadbolt or James Belich or Peter Jackson, somebody is going to walk over to me and ask if I used to be Michael King. And I, full of gratitude, knowing that this is as good as it gets, will answer yes, yes. And, I expect, I'll thank him for making an old writer happy.

12.

Literary Dunedin: An Outsider Looks In

A talk given in Dunedin during
The Robert Burns Fellowship, 1999

My determinedly North Island family was largely ignorant of Dunedin – I say 'largely' rather than 'wholly', because we did have books in which the city featured; we did know people who lived here; and my father had spent three months here prior to the war working for the now-extinct Radio Record, when he stayed in a George Street boarding house and went excavating caves at Victory Beach with David Teviotdale on weekends.

When I came to Dunedin for an NZUSA tournament and arts festival in 1965, it was the first time I had travelled south of the Marlborough Sounds. In that memorable week, I saw my first striptease, met Charles Brasch, and lost my virginity – not necessarily in that order. I'm not going to pander to prurience by telling you about the about the more intimate encounters. But I shall tell you about my one and only meeting with Charles Brasch.

It was late on a Saturday night and the party I was attending had run out of beer. Not even the flexible management practices of the Captain Cook or the Bowling Green would oblige us at that hour. Then one of our number, Tony Haas, like me a visitor from Wellington, said, 'Let's go and visit Charles Brasch. He's a poet. He'll be game for a drink or two.'

I should say that none of us in that small knot of students that beat its way up to Heriot Row had met Brasch previously. Tony knew the address because he had recently been in correspondence with Brasch over a *Salient* supplement on the arts in New Zealand. The rest of us knew him only as a poet and the editor of *Landfall.*

I should also say that in Wellington in the mid-1960s we had a rather different view of poets than that which may have prevailed in Dunedin. The city, our city, was still rife with legends about the prodigious drinking feats of Anton Vogt, Louis Johnson, Alistair Campbell, Brian Bell and the pre-teetotal Baxter. In our befuddled brains we imagined that Dunedin poets had comparable propensities: that Charles Brasch kept beer permanently on tap on Saturday nights for the literati; and that Ruth Dallas was probably a party girl of Beth Heke proportions.

Alas, we were mistaken. The first sign that all was not as we imagined was that all the lights were out at 36A Heriot Row. At this point, some of us began to lose courage and to suggest that, perhaps, we should abandon the expedition. But not Tony, who was nothing if not an optimist. 'Charlie's probably reading in bed,' he said. 'Bored rigid. He'll be thrilled to see us.' So we rang the bell. And waited. Then rang the bell some more and beat on the door as well, in case our putative host was hard of hearing.

At last a light went on inside. The door opened and a man stood there in slippers and some kind of embroidered oriental dressing gown. He looked exquisitely composed from the neck down. But his face, understandably it seems to me in retrospect, was wracked with alarm, and his eyes were blinking a lot, as if he was having difficulty focusing. 'Yes?' he asked. 'What's happened?'

'Nothing's happened,' Tony assured him, though I could see and hear even *his* confidence beginning to wane. 'I'm Tony Haas. From *Salient* in Wellington. We're at the student arts festival. We couldn't let a visit to Dunedin pass without saluting *Landfall* and its editor.' He paused to see what effect this was having. The expression on Brasch's face went from alarm to one of immense fatigue. There was a long moment of utter silence. Then he stepped back, holding the door open, and said, 'Well, you'd better come in.'

We had envisaged a keg on a Formica kitchen table over a lino floor. Instead we were shown into a living room which seemed to have an enormous number of original paintings, delicate ornaments and a plush carpet. We felt uncouth in our duffel coats and what we now recognised as presumptuous and vulgar behaviour. Our host disappeared for a moment, then returned with a round silver tray on which were half a dozen thimbles, each holding a minute quantity of sherry.

'Would you care for a drink?' he asked. We *cared.* We each seized a tiny glass and drained it, hoping, I suppose, that another injection of alcohol would numb the embarrassment that was now palpable. It did not. And once the drinks were gone there seemed nothing else to say or do. Even the voluble Tony was silenced. After a lengthy pause Brasch held out the tray and we replaced the glasses in a clatter. 'Well,' he said, 'it was kind of you to call. I'd better not detain you at this late hour.' 'No, no,' we all concurred. And practically fell over one another in an effort to get out the door.

I never had an opportunity to apologise to Charles Brasch for that unconscionable intrusion. By the time I was battering on *Landfall*'s door with short stories and essays, Brasch had retired and I was dealing with his successor, Robin Dudding.

There were a couple of later events that might loosely be considered sequels, however.

In May 1973 I was living back in Wellington after four years away from the city. On Friday nights I drank at the Duke of Edinburgh hotel, whose clientele was a blend of students, writers and criminals – with some patrons managing to belong simultaneously to all three categories.

One evening I fought my way into the crowded premises and jostled towards a table that included Alistair Campbell, Harry Orsman, Geoff Cochrane and Phillip Wilson. One of them intercepted me and told me to go up to the bar to collect my free drink. 'Who's shouting?' I wanted to know. 'The manager,' I was told. 'It's in honour of Charles Brasch. He's just died.' I was impressed. And moved. How many hotels in New Zealand – or elsewhere in the world, for that matter – would shout their patrons drinks when a poet died?

So I went to the bar and was handed a large pre-poured glass of Southern Comfort. Not my favourite tipple, but the supply of any drink free of charge off the top shelf was an occasion to remember and value. Later, when the manager himself showed up in the bar, I made a point of going over and shaking hands with him. 'I want to thank you for that tribute to Charles Brasch,' I said. 'That was a handsome gesture.' 'Charles Brasch?' he said, puckering up his face. 'Who's he? Never heard of him.' 'Well, your barman's handing out free drinks on the strength of Brasch's demise,' I said. 'Southern Comforts.' 'Good God,' he said, 'that's not for anybody called Brasch. That's because of the catastrophe. Haven't you heard? Janis Joplin's dead.'

Back at the writers' table, I didn't tell them. As Harry Orsman was saying at that very moment, there was a nice symmetry to drinking Southern Comfort in honour of somebody who had died in Dunedin. I didn't want to spoil that; nor the mood of elegiac reminiscence into which everybody had slipped. At least not until the following Friday's session.

The other sequel occurred far more recently, but related to something that happened in Dunedin shortly after that first visit of mine.

In 1966 Brasch retired as foundation editor of *Landfall*. Because the journal would subsequently be produced entirely from the Caxton premises in Christchurch, Brasch and Ruth Dallas closed down the Dunedin *Landfall* office above the University Bookshop in Great King Street. The furniture was dispersed. What to do with the famous *Landfall* desk? This was an eight-legged four-drawered monster with a surface only slightly smaller than the pitch at Carisbrook, which Brasch had bought cheaply at Browns.

At about the same time Janet Frame had just moved into the first house she owned, in Evans Street up the North East Valley, and she was in need of furniture. Brasch offered her the *Landfall* desk and she accepted it with gratitude. Like a Trojan horse, however, it brought problems. Carriers took a whole morning to get it into the house without removing external and internal doors. No sooner was it installed in the room designated as her study than Frame found it was too high for her to work at comfortably. So she took to all eight legs with a saw. Each time she thought she had amputated sufficiently the desk wobbled; so she took off a little more here; and a little more there. Eventually it resembled a dwarf's table. A very *large* dwarf's table, it's true. But a piece of furniture for little people nonetheless – a pavilion, perhaps, that they could crouch under. Worse, every time Frame entered or left the room the corners seemed to lunge at her and left bruises round her thighs and shins.

This close combat only came to an end when Frame decided to make an extended trip to the United States. While she was away she let her house to tenants, and her good friend Dorothy Neal White agreed to keep an eye on things. When Frame returned, she was met at Dunedin

Station by a white-faced Neal White, who told her to brace herself for bad news. It was the *Landfall* desk, she said. The tenants had not been able to fit their bed into the room, nor get the desk out. So they had sliced it in half, roughly, not expertly, and stored both sections in the basement. Frame, vastly amused, tried to take this seriously so as not to offend her friend.

Home again, Frame retrieved the desk from the basement, propped its two halves together, and continued to work at it, on a chair that had to be cut down to accommodate the reduced height. Everybody who saw the desk agreed that it looked grotesque, not to say downright ugly. But Frame continued to use it for its single overwhelming virtue: the acreage of its surface, which accommodated every scrap of paper on which she was working. When she left Dunedin she carted it to Whangaparaoa, Glenfield, Stratford, Wanganui and Levin. When she got to Levin she tired of its size and discomfort and the difficulties associated with moving it, and gave it away to next door neighbours. That, she thought with relief, was that.

It was not. Last year a letter reached me from Wellington conservation architect Chris Cochran. Victoria University, he told me, had just acquired an important literary artefact. He had been commissioned to establish its provenance and to write a report on how to restore and preserve it for posterity. The artefact in question was a desk, allegedly associated with some of New Zealand's most enduringly valuable works of literature, and it had been donated to the university by a Mrs Giselle McCashin of Levin.

'The desk has several curious features,' he continued. 'The most dramatic is that it is in two pieces. The surface, including the leatherette, has been sawn through . . . the cuts were made from one side, and then the other, and they don't quite meet. The legs have been cut down unevenly, apparently to reduce the height of the desk. There is a large red ink stain on the right-hand side of the leatherette, which is loose around the edges and torn. Anything you can tell me about the origin of these fabric features would be gratefully received; clearly, they constitute a visible record of the desk's history and ownership.'

Indeed. I did the requested research and passed on the information. And I have since learned that a word processor Janet Frame gave away to an impoverished would-be writer in Dunedin has been reverently placed in an attic, where it is shown to visitors and its features pointed out in hushed tones. Like a medieval saint, it seems, Janet Frame is going to find it difficult to dispose of rubbish.

All I've said thus far relates to my casual brushes with the *real* Dunedin – or, to put it more soberly, with aspects of literary Dunedin of which I have had passing experiential knowledge.

Beyond *that* reality, however, there is another Dunedin: a *virtual* Dunedin which I have encountered and continue to encounter in literature. And it was this literary Dunedin that I knew long before I came here in person; and which I still feel I know more intimately, perhaps, than the city and community which throbs away beyond the walls of this building.

I grew up a solitary child in a household that was not bookish, but was *full* of books. In particular it was full of *New Zealand* books. Imprints such as Whitcombe and Tombs, Caxton and Blackwood and Janet Paul were as familiar to me as 'clean burning Europa, the petrol with pep' and 'Weetbix with hot milk, popular with everyone'. I had read my way through the entire collection, including the forbidden 'adult books' on the top shelf, by the time I was fifteen. Then was simply a question of keeping up with new volumes as they arrived.

Three of those books gave me, in totum, a sense of what Dunedin might be like. We had a copy of *Children of the Poor* by John A. Lee, given to us by my father's old naval buddy, Phil Connolly, who was also a Dunedin MP. We had Jess Whitworth's *Otago Interval,* which my father had bought because of his association with her first husband,

Roger Duff, whose *Listener* absorbed his *Radio Record.* And we got an inscribed copy of Denis Glover's *Hot Water Sailor* the week it appeared, because Denis was a family friend – or had been until the disastrous year in which he worked – or, rather, didn't work – in my father's advertising agency.

Lee's *roman-à-clef* offered what Dorothy Neal White called 'an uncommissioned portrait' of Otago and Dunedin. Uncommissioned, perhaps, and rejected vociferously when it appeared. But for me, a schoolboy reading on the shores of a temperate North Island estuary, it was a vivid depiction of a place that seemed both harsher and hardier than the one in which I lived.

Jess Whitworth's *Otago Interval* had won a national writing competition sponsored by the Progressive Publishing Society in 1945. That very year the society collapsed, however, and was unable to publish its prize-winning novel. It was Blackwood and Janet Paul who brought it out five years later. Like Lee, Whitworth's autobiographical heroine Lou Brodie experiences turn-of-the-century Dunedin. But her city is very different from that described by Albany Porcello. Whitworth's character lives and moves on the hills above the city, in locations such as London Street and Arthur Street rather than the slums of Hanover and Albany streets. As others have noted, her autobiographical book is redolent with specific period details – the vivid textures of social history.

Denis Glover, too, attended and wrote, in *Hot Water Sailor*, about Arthur Street School, the same institution Janet Frame would describe walking out of a generation later – making it, perhaps, a competitor with Waitaki Boys High and Sacred Heart College in Auckland for the title of New Zealand school with the most heavyweight literary associations.

My next literary encounters with Dunedin occurred at secondary school. I did my first two years at Sacred Heart College in Auckland, where my English teacher, Brother Stephen, had taught Dan Davin,

Michael Joseph and Maurice Duggan. He was a good teacher and an early evangelist for New Zealand writing; and he drew our attention to three books in the college library in which Dunedin featured.

One was Davin's novel *Cliffs of Fall,* named for the cliffs at St Clair, which Dorothy Neal White called Dunedin's *Crime and Punishment.* We also read, at Brother Stephen's instigation, A. P. Gaskell's fiction in *The Big Game and Other Stories.* It included, of course, that wonderful title piece in which Carisbrook, that hallowed ground, is itself a character in the story.

Brother Stephen had a particular enthusiasm for E. H. McCormick. We were given cyclostyled extracts from *Letters and Art in New Zealand,* in blatant breach of copyright. And those of us who were interested were allowed to borrow *The Inland Eye,* a slight publication which had begun life as a public lecture, and urged to study it as a model of autobiographical writing. And what a model it was, with its exquisite miniature portraits of Taihape, Wellington and Dunedin, all put to good use when Dennis McEldowney assembled McCormick's posthumous autobiography, *An Absurd Ambition,* a couple of years ago.

Those, then, were some of the images of Dunedin I grew up with, and remembered, and sometimes returned to reread. But really, the best was yet to come. The most telling literary glimpses of the city and its life were eventually to be found in the Burns Fellowship poetry of James K. Baxter, the poetry, fiction and autobiographies of Janet Frame, and the autobiography of Charles Brasch.

I suggested earlier that I knew this virtual Dunedin, preserved in the amber of our literature, rather better than I know physical Dunedin. That certainly *was* the case. But it's rather less so with every day that passes. Because in this *annus mirabilis* of the Burns Fellowship I am slowly tracing the literary footprints and re-placing them, or at the very least accompanying them, with first-hand experiences of places and people which had existed formerly only in my imagination.

Thus I walk past Willi Fels's Manono, stop and stare at it; and as I do so my mind's eye provides images of the young Charles Brasch coming and going, accompanied, perhaps, by his sister Lel or his de Beer cousins. I stroll up Carroll Street, note the absence of Garden Terrace, where Janet Frame lived with Uncle George and Aunty Isy and scoffed all the prize chocolates. And I carry on up the hill to the Southern Cemetery, where she hid her menstrual rags and sat and stared at the city and wondered what would become of her. And I stride up London Street to contemplate the house where Jess Whitworth played with her friend Fanny, daughter of the rabbi, and encountered there a world both more feral and more exotic than any she knew in her home life.

Dunedin, it seems to me, is especially blessed in two respects.

One is that it features more frequently in literature than any other New Zealand city. It is our own modest equivalent of London, which reverberates all the more for us because of the preserved words of Donne, Johnson, Dickens, Hazlitt and Lamb.

The other blessing, fortuitous *and* fortunate, is that the city's sequence of gold-and wool-induced prosperity produced a solid Victorian and Edwardian city, which its subsequent *lack* of prosperity largely preserved. Dunedin is physically and culturally more intact than any other New Zealand city because it lacked their incentive to destroy and rebuild; to shed old skins and grow new ones. Dunedin's umbilical cord is still visibly attached to its navel.

And this miracle permits another. It allows anyone who wants to, to reconcile literary and modern Dunedin, to linger in streets and in front of houses where the past seems close to the present, and the psychic residue of people who went before us still seems palpable.

It also allows me to reread with particular delight the accounts of Dunedin I first read as a child and adolescent. Because now they have a pleasing familiarity that is a sediment from those initial readings, recognising what one encounters without remembering what comes next; and that familiarity is further animated by recent and *actual* experience of those places. And in this way do our own lives link with literature and generate that especially delicious frisson which Proust encapsulated in his marvellous expression, 'À la recherche du temps perdu' – remembrance of things past.

And all this in turn allows me to stand in front of 36A Heriot Row and ask the shade of Charles Brasch forgiveness for a display of bad manners thirty-three years ago.

13.

A Life Touched by Angels and Shadows

2004

Janet Frame, who died in her home town of Dunedin this week, was unquestionably the most decorated writer this country has produced. In addition to winning every literary prize for which she was eligible in New Zealand, most recently the inaugural Prime Minister's Award for Achievement in Fiction in 2003, she was a member of the American Academy of Arts and Letters, recipient of a Commonwealth Prize for Literature, and holder of Italian and Chilean awards. She also won civil honours – a CBE and membership of the Order of New Zealand – and honorary doctorates and medals from a cluster of universities.

And all this for a relatively modest output over fifty years of twelve novels, four story collections, one collection of poetry and three volumes of autobiography. The big one, the Nobel Prize for Literature, eluded her. But the fact that she was on the shortlist at least twice, in 1998 and 2003, was proof that her achievement was taken seriously in the world of international literary criticism right up to the time of her death.

Frame herself, however, was untouched by the notion that she was a genius and a world-renowned writer. People could *say* it; that didn't make it so. To her, her reputation was but one of many features of existence which she found surreal and even preposterous – like the very fact of being alive, or of daring to use language to capture and convey human experience. Asked about such things, she tended to say, 'Oh well . . .' and trail off into silence. In the end you accepted that these sorts of questions, like inquiries about her writing, were simply off-limits.

It would of course have been impossible to have known Frame without an awareness of how important writing was to her. 'I think it's all that matters to me,' she once told Frank Sargeson, 'I dread emerging from it each day.' And it was in the act of writing that she daily renewed her identity and sense of purpose, even in the last decade of her life when she released nothing new for publication beyond a handful of poems.

In the wake of her autobiographies and the Jane Campion film based on them that popularised a knowledge of her early life and work, she had sufficient income on which to live from the increased sale of her existing books. There was no incentive to publish additional volumes. Almost certainly, however, there will be work eventually available for posthumous publication – poems, of which she wrote literally thousands; and the manuscripts of at least two novels, if she turns out to have resisted the temptation to destroy them.

For friends and family, however, writing will not be at the head of the list of things they will remember about her. For one thing, they never saw her do it. She was only able to function at the keyboard if there was nobody else in the house. That was why she lived alone by choice, and why unscheduled or unknown visitors wreaked havoc on her creative life.

No, what those who knew her will recall most vividly is her intense and immense compassion for people who were marginalised or in any respect – financially, physically or emotionally – worse off than herself. This concern was one which spilled over from life into her literature. Just occasionally, it made her vulnerable to conmen (I once, to my horror, heard her offer to lend all her savings to someone who proposed to invest them in a highly risky film venture); more often, it led her to sponsor the work of talented but unconfident young artists who had appealed to her for help.

Her second most memorable quality was her quirkiness, her ability to view aspects of life in a manner that was, for conventional people, slightly off-key, but always apt. 'That was a very "Janet" thing to say,' was the expression most often used in recounting conversations with her. Asked last year, when she was already ill with leukaemia, if she found it difficult to inspect the local hospice on the same day she learned that she was once again on the Nobel Prize shortlist, she replied, 'Not at all. It accords well with my sense of drama.' And as she entered Dunedin Hospital for treatment of the advanced disease, she was delighted to read the warning notice on the door of her room. It said 'Protective Isolation'. 'That's what I've been in all my life!' she chortled.

Part of her quirkiness extended to a brilliant flair for language that was, of course, a feature of her fiction and poetry. But it also revealed itself when she was 'at play'. To take her on in Scrabble, for example, was to be exposed to the full force of her linguistic facility and memory. It was also to come up against her powers of invention. 'What does "silltits" mean?' we asked on one occasion, when she offloaded all her letters on to somebody else's 'S' to create an unlikely combination. 'It's what all those women in New York get,' she said, 'when they spend all day leaning out of tenement windows and watching the action in the street.' On the strength of that explanation, she was allowed the word. And she won the game, as she almost always did.

The quirkiness was also apparent in telephone conversations and messages. 'Hello? This is . . . Janet!' she would say when she rang, beginning with a greeting that sounded like a question, then announcing her name after a pause, as if it was as much a surprise to her as it was to the recipient. Her answerphone messages were marvellous exercises in stream-of-consciousness existentialism. 'Hello? I'm not here. Oh! . . . I mustn't say that. I *might* be here. Anyway, please leave a message.'

One of the jokes she most enjoyed was the fact that her telephone number was a closely guarded secret, to be divulged only to those who knew her or had legitimate business to discuss with her. And yet, wherever she lived, there was her telephone number in the local directory listed under 'Clutha, Janet', the name she had adopted by deed poll in London in 1958. (The whole of that new name was 'Nene Janet Paterson Clutha' – Nene for the Ngapuhi chief Tamati Waka Nene, whom she had admired from her schoolgirl reading of *Our Nation's Story*, Paterson for her Scottish grandmother, and Clutha in honour of the mighty Otago river; the computer-generated letters she knew she could safely ignore were those that began, presumptuously and ignorantly, 'Dear Nene'.)

The whole episode of the name change and its ramifications were characteristic of Frame. She wanted the casually known people among whom she dwelt to know her as Janet Clutha, in order that they might *not* know that she was 'Janet Frame, the famous writer'. It worked in London from 1958 to 1963. It scarcely ever worked in New Zealand, where for many years her iconic halo of bushy red hair gave her away, even if the name Clutha did not.

She also enjoyed the confusions that her naming strategy produced: her status as possibly the only writer in the world to *live* under a nom de plume and *write* under her own name; and the announcement from a Minister of Internal Affairs that the 1964 Scholarship in Letters had been awarded to 'Miss Janet Frame from Clutha', a non-existent New Zealand place name.

While all kinds of stories have and will be told about Frame's eccentricities, her reputation will not be sullied by the sorts of revelations that have soiled the memory of Dame Iris Murdoch. It's true that for Frame, like Murdoch, housekeeping and cleaning were not high priorities and that every house into which she moved rapidly took on the appearance of a slum (one visitor, Liz Calder of the London publishing house Bloomsbury, carefully carried the fresh scones Frame had baked for her to her next engagement and buried them in Maurice Shadbolt's garden in the erroneous belief that they might harbour dangerous pathogens). In fact, while Frame's kitchens and bathrooms were untidy, they were never dirty. Nobody endangered their lives by visiting them.

Domestic disorganisation, though, did seem to shorten the lives of the household of office appliances she loved to buy. In Palmerston North she acquired a photocopier. But the amount of space it commandeered in the living room and the fact that it gave off toxic fumes persuaded her to banish it to the garage, where it became infested with ants looking for a warm dry place in which to nest. For weeks all of Frame's photocopied letters and manuscript pages emerged speckled with squashed insects. Even when she had the machine serviced and cleaned, *images* of ants continued to appear on the copied pages. Then the machine broke down completely and she gave it away.

She told this story with relish, as she did the one about the ugly, mutilated *Landfall* desk, which she managed to fob off on to a Levin neighbour, only to see it resurrected as a precious literary relic in the creative writing room at Victoria University. As a writer, she took it for granted that life was made up of an interconnected network of stories, and that telling them was the way we made sense of the world and redeemed its harsher realities with humour.

For myself, I will always respect and admire Janet Frame's published writing with its profound insights into the conflicts we all experience between creation and destruction, love and hate, hope and fear. But the friend I miss will be the one who, confronted by the bare floorboards of Frank Sargeson's house, gave in to an irresistible urge to tap dance – and did so with her eyes glinting with mischief and fun.

The fact is that, in addition to being the consummate artist justly decorated with global honours, Janet Frame was also that most recognisable of New Zealand institutions: a real dag. And *that* phenomenon, the Orsman *Dictionary of New Zealand English* reminds us, is someone 'extraordinary or entertaining, amusingly eccentric or impudent, a character, a hard case.' Janet Frame was *all* these things. And she will be greatly missed.

14.

Janet and the Birds

A speech given at Janet Frame's memorial service, 2004

First, some rapid acknowledgements:

There was something Janet said to me in the course of writing the biography that I feel sure she would want me to repeat on this occasion. 'I might well be a Frame,' she said, 'but when I want help it's a Gordon for me every time.' She was referring, of course, to the fact that among the many people who helped to sustain her – all the angels at her tables alongside the Frank Sargesons and Charles Brasches and Bob Cawleys and Bill Browns – her longest-serving and most faithful support team over a period of almost six decades were her sister June and brother-in-law Wilson Gordon. And she relished the fact that one of those shifts of language in which she took so much pleasure had given a whole new meaning to the song and dance in praise of the doughty and virile clan into which her sister had married: the 'Gay Gordons'. Janet was also thrilled and proud that she lived long enough to see the publication last year of June's own first book.

In the past four months, the member of the Frame/Gordon clan who looked after Janet with heroic courage and stamina was Pamela – who ensured among much else that Janet was able to remain in the familiarity and comfort of her own home to within two days of her death. We salute you and thank you, Pamela; and June and Wilson, to whom we owe a debt, as Janet herself did, for the fact that the person whom we honour today emerged and flourished as a writer like no other.

A little over two weeks ago something extraordinary occurred in and to New Zealand. A writer died, and it seemed as if the whole country held its breath and then let out a collective sigh. 'Nation Loses Its Voice', ran the headline in *The Australian*. And here, Janet's passing and its significance was noted in newspaper stories, features, editorials, even cartoons, and in massive radio and television commentary. The *Listener* decided, at last, to make of her a cover story. And all this, like the overseas bulletins and obituaries, reverberated with regret, respect, admiration. For me, though, the impact of Janet's passing, and its unprecedented force, was most apparent in the number of people I didn't know, 'ordinary people', one might say, who stopped me in the streets of Hamilton that week, and in the corridors of Waikato Hospital, to say how bereaved they felt. And they used the first person plural – 'We've lost that wonderful woman' – to indicate a sense of national possession and of national loss, and I think a feeling that they had lost part of themselves.

All this was a measure of the unprecedented extent to which a writer had imprinted herself on the consciousness of her country. Those orphaned by her disappearance were responding not to the designations 'world-famous writer' or 'Nobel Prize contender', but to the loss of someone who had found a way to make her solitary heart bridge the gaps that otherwise divide people. They were moved especially by the resonance of her own life story: that of a woman who through tragic circumstances lost control of her life; and then, as a consequence of immense strength and courage, regained that life and her possession of it. It's not simply a fundamental New Zealand story; it is, ultimately, the most powerful of human stories.

However! I'm not going to speak today as Janet's biographer. I've been doing that in a variety of forums for the past fortnight. I want instead to speak of her as fellow writer and friend, and to do so by recounting a couple of short episodes, about Janet and birds. They come into the category of what she herself, alive, called 'private stuff'. But, as the writer in her always acknowledged, it's the 'private stuff' that is revealing of character and sensibility, in this case Janet's own. And Janet was not only a person who told stories: she was one around whom stories accumulated.

'We confer value on life,' Janet once wrote, 'by feeling deeply each other's mortality.' Over the past four months, she and I found an additional bond in the fact that news of our respective illnesses was confirmed on the same day. From that point our conversations focused on the health and progress of the other, rather than on our own symptoms. And an awareness of the possible proximity of death made Janet exquisitely aware of the potential meanings of portents in both of our lives.

In October 2003, Maria and I were visited at home by Peter Harrison, Joanna Paul's recently widowed husband. We were speaking of the utterly tragic circumstances surrounding her death. I went to fetch a small watercolour Joanna had done for me years before and returned to find Maria and Peter in a state of high excitement. 'You've just missed the most extraordinary thing,' Peter said.

Our living room looks out on to bush, with a large-leafed parapara in the foreground. No sooner had I left the room than a morepork, in full daylight, had cannoned into the tree and clung there on a swaying branch, side-on to the window. Then, as Peter and Maria watched, the bird turned its head to one side and looked directly at them, seeming to hold their gaze through the window for a full minute. Then it shook itself and took off.

In my conversation with Janet that night, there arose the question of what this might mean; and in particular what it might mean in my then current circumstance, with the presence of malignant tumours just confirmed in my throat and my neck. Janet, who usually spoke of consulting Jacquie Baxter on such matters, this time made an immediate diagnosis. Or, rather, she made several.

'It could be a sign,' she said, 'that we're both going to die. Or that one of us is going to die.' 'Well', I said, 'that has to be me. The bird came to my house.' 'No it didn't,' she went on. 'The owl came looking for you. And you weren't there. And it shook its head. That might mean you're reprieved.' 'Or you are,' I said. 'No,' she said, 'I don't think so.' And then: 'We'll see . . .' And 'we'll see' was Janet's customary expression for curtailing an immediate conversational topic but leaving it open for revisitation.

Most of us are familiar with Janet's story, her first story, in which the hawk flies out of the sky and eats the birdie – 'oh poor little birdie.' But it would be wrong to let the character of today's gathering leave the impression that Janet saw birds – especially New Zealand birds, which, she believed, expressed the soul of the country, having lived here so much longer than people – that she saw them only as messengers of ominous portent. One of her most treasured memories was the spectacle of fantails and silvereyes confiding in her mother at Willowglen.

So let me end with another cameo more representative of Janet's whole life. Late one afternoon in her living room in St Kilda she put a finger to her lips and said, 'Come with me.' She led me through the front door and out to the gate on the street, and we stood there. 'What?'

I asked. 'Listen,' she said. And then came the sound, from a lone tree across the road: the clear notes of a bellbird up and down the scale. 'A bellbird sang in Melbourne Street,' she said in her marvelling, slightly breathless mode. 'Vera Lynn, huh?' I responded. 'No,' she said. 'No . . . Hopkins, Gerard Manley Hopkins.'

Apart from the tree, that aspect of Melbourne Street was a severe little corridor of concrete and asphalt and metal railings. Surveying it, and still hearing the bird, Janet began to recite:

> And for all this, nature is never spent;
> There lives the dearest freshness deep down things . . .

I joined her for the next couplet:

> And, though the last lights off the black west went,
> Oh, morning, at the brown brink eastward springs!

And as we sprang together, she laughed and her eyes danced in that inward-sun smile that dissolved her septuagenarian face into that of a seven-year-old.

That will be for me – the woman who always took delight in the rediscovery that life and literature could make sense of each other, and who shared and spread that delight – that will be my most abiding memory of her.

Go in peace, Janet, and take with you our love and our gratitude. And, to quote your beloved Hopkins, 'God rest you all road ever you offended.'

15.

Remembering Dan and Winnie Davin

2000

A memoirist as accomplished as Dan Davin deserves remembrance in essays characterised by seamless narrative and sensibility. For a variety of reasons, including the pre-existence of Keith Ovenden's magisterial biography, what follows is simply a patchwork of recollections, diary notes and letter fragments.

I met Dan Davin the same week that I met Iris Murdoch, Stephen Spender and John Lehmann. He stayed in touch; they, unsurprisingly, did not. All four encounters occurred in the course of the forty-first International PEN Congress in London in August 1976. Dan was not a conference delegate. Eric McCormick, who was, suggested I accompany him to the University Tavern in Bloomsbury to meet Dan, up from Oxford on an overnight visit.

Having read all of Dan's published fiction and his war history volume on Crete, and knowing something of his status as one of the world's leading academic publishers and unofficial high commissioner for New Zealand culture in Britain, I approached the meeting with considerable awe. Possibly as a consequence of this, I made a poor impression. I upset a pint of bitter into the lap of his friend Martha McCulloch, who bawled out 'Capital S, H, one T' and then refused to sit next to me. And I was introduced by Dan to some later arrivals as 'the well-known New Zealand writer Maurice Shadbolt'.

It was in part to compensate for these blunders, perhaps, and to lift my sagging spirits that Dan invited me to visit him and Winnie in Oxford when I was due to return to England from the Continent four months later. I did, and the second encounter was redolent of warmth and charm.

I joined them at the Gardener's Arms on a winter's evening shortly before Christmas. Dan presided over a cheerful drinking school that included the anthropologists Godfrey and Peter Lienhardt and others from the university and 'the Press'. The only topic of conversation I recall was a disorderly attempt to construct the Great New Zealand Novel from the title *The Mutton Bird Flies*. Later we went home to Southmoor Road for supper and – much later – sleep. I was shown to a bed into which, I was given to understand, Dylan Thomas had preceded me on more than one occasion.

Diary notes written on the train back to London register my impression at the time:

> He has the refined air of a squire, sonorous voice, dark good looks, and is lightly erudite. One of those people who become more attractive as they age. He is at ease in Oxford, being clever and donnish in a place where the things he values are valued. Small-town New Zealand life (Invercargill, Dunedin) did not value these things: literature, the life

of the mind, liberality . . .

His routine is invariable. Up early, makes tea, reads *The Times*, does the crossword, then takes Winnie tea and toast in bed. They don't talk at this hour. After work he presides at the Gardener's Arms like a priest. His group has its own table, Dan sits at the head. Peter Lienhardt tells me that the chair remains empty on the evenings Dan is not there and the rest of them feel directionless. He says also that Dan has a drinking 'problem' – but there was no sign of that in his behaviour, other than a spreading and contagious mellowness . . .

Dan says he likes Iris Murdoch but not her books ('Take all the sordidness, perversion and freakishness you can dredge out of the imagination and you have a Murdoch novel'). He prefers to read and write mannered fiction. In some senses Dan himself keeps writing the same book, or at least returns to the kinds of considerations that one feels arise from his own life . . .

Winnie was the surprise, perhaps because I had no prior knowledge and therefore no expectations of her. She is chubby and bright-eyed, embracing and embracable. And as sharp – perhaps sharper – in conversation. She was the most vivacious raconteur at the table. Her relations with the likes of Joyce Cary and Dylan T. seem to have been quite separate from Dan's. She's more recognisably 'New Zealand' than Dan. But is no less confident for that. Perhaps more so?

I saw them again on a further short visit to Oxford in January 1977; and Dan sent me off with an inscribed copy of *Brides of Price*. Over the next twenty months we exchanged letters about books and literary gossip. Dan sent news of New Zealanders in the UK (Fleur Adcock, Kevin Ireland, Bruce and Elspeth Purchase); and of his effort to disengage from the Clarendon Press ('I had hoped to fade out like the Cheshire Cat over my last year; instead I'll be jumping about like a scalded cat on hot bricks').

In August 1978 Dan and Winnie were in New Zealand in the course of Dan's swansong tour for Oxford University Press. We got together for lunch in Wellington; and, subsequently, to allow me to record interviews with him for the *Listener* and the Concert Programme. At Dan's suggestion, I attempted to charge the lunch to Radio New Zealand and received a stringent dressing down from the producer of the books programme ('This is Wellington, you know, not Shepherd's Bush. We don't do this sort of thing, not even for people from Oxford').

Some extracts from the radio interview, Dan speaking:

> On the whole I tend to back the All Blacks, unless they're playing Ireland. I'm not a strong nationalist of any sort. But I'm capable of nationalist sentiments if they happen to correspond with my subjective harmonies. So that sometimes one feels like an Irishman, sometimes an Englishman, sometimes a New Zealander. On the whole, more often the last.
>
> But when I come back to New Zealand I see that I am not really a New Zealander in the current sense. They seem to talk without listening, they eat more than I can ever eat, they drink abominable beer, they argue politics in what seems to me to be slightly scurrilous and excessively vehement personalia, instead of speaking to the point at issue [these were the years of the Muldoon prime ministership] . . .
>
> I think there's been an enormous change in New Zealand writing since the war. Writers seem to be able to find outlets for serious short stories and poems that were not available in my time. Had they been, I might have thought of coming back . . . I've just been reading a book of Vincent O'Sullivan's, *The Boy, the Bridge and the River*. It really is as good as anything I've seen coming out of New Zealand . . . I've also been struck by the novels of Maurice Gee . . . They seem to have gathered in power and experience to quite an extraordinary degree . . .

[When] I was last here in 1969 I was at a literary party in Dunedin. I was struck by the way that people . . . were now not talking of T. S. Eliot or D. H. Lawrence or outside reference of that sort as they would have been in my time, but . . . in terms of their own writers, James K. Baxter and Charles Brasch and so on . . . There had built up a sufficient stock of indigenous art on which they could draw and I felt this was a very healthy change.

Katherine Mansfield, if she were writing a letter to somebody now, would not be able to say, 'I want to make my undiscovered country leap into the eyes of the Old World' – because, first, she wouldn't care so much about the Old World, and secondly because her country would not be 'undiscovered' for the generations of artists who'd preceded her.

I asked him about Lawrence Jones's description of him as a 'sceptical post-Christian writer with a tragic view of life':

It sounds an absurdly pompous phrase taken out of a less pompous context. But curiously enough I think I would half go along with it, which means I almost agree with it. And as I only half agree with anything I say myself, that's a fairly high standard to apply . . . Puritanism? Permissiveness is itself a response to puritanism, and is therefore in itself puritan . . . I think in criticism of my own work the word puritanism is used much too simply. Because Irish puritanism is quite different from, say, Presbyterian puritanism. I would have thought that Sargeson would have balanced out the view that Irish puritanism was the only brand in New Zealand . . .

In the *Listener* piece, I noted that his conversation 'reveals a wit that is both wry and dry, a weakness for puns and a fondness for allusion. One detects a tussle between the obligations to declare what is true and reasonable and the temptation to say what is clever or amusing . . .

What he says is frequently both reasonable and amusing. He thrives on talk and is disappointed by people who don't respond in kind. He has likened one associate [Michael Joseph] to a tennis player who reacts to a vigorous service simply by smiling and pocketing the ball.'

There was an odd sequel to these interviews. I had a letter from James Bertram which complimented me on both, but took strong exception to my depiction of Dan as 'elegant in an absent-minded way'. 'That bit is sheer fantasy,' wrote Bertram. 'Dan is the least elegant person I have ever met.' I was surprised and wondered how often they had met.

I didn't see the Davins again until February and March 1981, when I returned to the United Kingdom for preliminary research on a biography of Peter Fraser – a subject that, because of his war experience and authorship of the *Crete* volume, interested Dan rather more than my previous projects.

The beginning of the first visit, in February, seemed jinxed. On the London tube, en route for the Paddington train that would carry me to Oxford, my shoulder bag was slit open and my passport, travellers' cheques, credit cards and money stolen. I arrived in Oxford cashless and distressed. We gathered again in a pub, this time the Horse and Jockey (Dan's group was in dispute with the publican at the Gardener's Arms over some slight). In the course of the evening I left the table to use the toilet. Hanging on the back of my chair was the unusually smart and expensive quilted skiing jacket I had bought in Nice the previous week, to insulate myself from what was proving to be a tenaciously cold European winter. While I was absent, Dan pushed the chair aside to allow somebody laden with drinks to pass. The right arm of the jacket brushed the gas fire and the sleeve ignited.

On my way back to the table I could smell the acrid stench of burning nylon. I discovered the company exhilarated and my fashion-plate jacket on the floor, trampled, soaked in ale and ashes and minus one arm. Dan had risen to the occasion magnificently, Godfrey Lienhardt reported. It was as if he were back in Crete, under fire. As soon as the flame flared he kicked the chair over, stamped on the burning sleeve and called for liquid. One by one he poured pints of beer on to the jacket until the whole garment was sodden. Then he announced that the crisis was over and that no doubt I would want to show my appreciation by getting the next round. Cashless and now coatless in a foreign country – a cold foreign country – I did not recover until we had eaten a supper of braised chops at Southmoor Road.

In the course of the second visit, a month later, Dan took me to lunch at his college, Balliol, which was every bit as dignified and graceful as I had imagined. Appropriately enough, we talked about Evelyn Waugh and Dan commented that *Brideshead Revisited* was 'theologically coherent but artistically flawed'.

That evening Winnie cut short the drinking time to announce that we had to return home at once to watch 'something on television'. I assumed it was one of the highly regarded BBC Two programmes on art or literature that I had heard so much about and looked forward to a night of high culture and elevated discussion, which would nicely complement the Balliol visit. The programme in question turned out to be *Starsky and Hutch*. Winnie followed the action with the rapt attention – and the exclamations – of a Southland supporter at a Ranfurly Shield game. Indeed, we all watched as we ate, and added a modicum of ribald commentary. It was an immensely happy evening.

I never saw Dan again. We continued to correspond, initially about Peter Fraser (whom he had met when the Prime Minister visited the New Zealand Division in Italy in 1944); and more latterly about Dan's fellow intelligence officer on Freyberg's staff, Paddy Costello. Dan was writing a memoir of Costello, who had died in 1963 but came to the attention of Western media in 1981 because of accusations in a book by Chapman Pincher (*Their Trade is Treachery*) that Costello had spied for the Russians while he worked as a New Zealand diplomat in

Moscow and Paris after the war. Some extracts from Dan's letters of that period:

> By that stage of the war [May 1944] we soldiers had developed a rather childishly arrogant attitude towards politicians who turned up when things were going well and there was no danger . . . Peter Fraser was well liked and respected. The sort of reaction I give was not unlike that of awful blasphemy in Catholic countries: it is only possible when the faith is thriving.
>
> I do not for a moment believe Paddy was a spy. He left the CP, I rather think, in 1940 or 1939 because of that nonsense about its being a capitalist war. It was at that time that he joined the NZ Div as a private. He was about the best linguist I have ever known and learnt Russian from a White Russian [woman] in Cairo . . . This was when, after a superb performance as a lance-corporal in 21 Bn in Greece, Freyberg had him sent to an OCTU in Cairo and that was when we first became friends . . .
>
> The CIA kept chasing the NZ Govt to sack him because of his CP associations and because he did not conceal his Russian sympathies and his contempt for much that was American. On the other hand, I remember his telling me of his frustration when he was warning the NZ Govt that the Russians had a [hydrogen] bomb when no-one else, least of all the Americans, would believe him . . . it was like being a military intelligence officer whose general would pay no attention to his reports . . . P was very black in his cups, not a good drinker: I had many a physical struggle with him as well as argumentative – he was a master of detecting what to say which would hurt your feelings most. This accounts for many of his sayings that mortally wounded the earnest and unimaginative Americans.

Later letters increasingly took on the appearance of medical bulletins:

> Thanks for the good wishes for the back operation . . . Pain is negligible, surgeon thinks he was wonderful, I think I was wonderful as well as the surgeon, atheists have been restored to a belief in God, the pious have been reinforced in their views about the power of Satan, and Winnie seems rather relieved. Too early yet to say how much mobility has been restored; enough, for the moment, to be able to say that I can walk to and from the Gardener's Arms without contravening my promise to the surgeon that I would not walk more than half a mile . . .

Later still:

> My shingles has pretty well gone and the accompanying and stifling depression. I dig away at the garden without undue pain and managed to fall off a ladder a few days ago without a bruise. I was delighted to find I could still fall and roll away from it as after a Rugby tackle . . . All I need back now is my libido and some 40 years. But I get the latter by becoming more and more soaked in the Div – which is rather absurd – and I reconcile myself to the loss of the former by hardly noticing its departure and having to waste less energies in endless schemes of outwitry and telling lies.

A last opportunity to meet in Auckland in January 1985 was lost when first I was ill and then Dan hospitalised with a perforated ulcer. Now, I sensed, he was too sick and lacking in stamina to enjoy correspondence. I ceased to write, except when I had a specific query, such as permission to cite his letters from Frank Sargeson for that biography. News of his death in 1990 came as a shock. It was not until I read the Ovenden book that I grasped just how full those final years were of depression and illness, just as the earlier years had been filled to such an extraordinary degree with work and friendship and promotion of New Zealand cultural interests in Britain.

He was not an imaginative writer of the first rank, though his Southland stories made him the social historian of New Zealand Irish-Catholic culture and his war fiction takes us closer than any other source to experiencing life in the Second Division of the New Zealand Army in North Africa and Italy. His *Crete* volume is the best-written of the war histories. For me, his breadth and his humanity were encapsulated in the epigraph he wrote for *The Salamander and the Fire*, his collected war stories: 'To those who, out of principle, refused to fight, and suffered for it. And to those who fought so that, among much else, that principle should be safeguarded.'

The other quality I cherished in him was one that older New Zealand writers ascribed to Sargeson. Dan was a point of contact for us with the wider world of English letters, culture and politics. He wrote obituaries for *The Times* and reviews for the *TLS*. He gave one a strong sense of the literary life, with its effluvia of letters, manuscripts, books, periodicals and gossip. He knew things about famous writers – Cary, Thomas, MacNeice, A. J. P. Taylor – that were not commonplace knowledge; and he knew them because he knew the writers. His correspondence was routinely littered with phrases such as, 'I'll ask Isaiah Berlin about that when I next see him'; or, 'Jon Stallworthy's talking to Anthony Blunt next week – we'll see what he thinks'.

Winnie, of course, remained, so contact with Southmoor Road did not end at once. She answered queries about Sargeson, and about Sargeson and Dan, incisively and by return mail. Indeed, she turned out to be every bit as elegant and entertaining a correspondent as Dan. Her letters too had the kinds of telling comments and anecdotes that give resonance to a correspondence:

> [Frank] decided in the early evening that he would feed us all, and got beautiful vegetables from his garden. He wouldn't let any of us help, but he told me and Wendy Purdie to sit on high stools by his counter

> and talk to him while he prepared vegetables etc. Amiable chat, and then he waved an enormous corn cob at me and said, 'Doesn't this remind you of Dan?' 'No,' I said, 'of William Faulkner.' Frank said, 'You can come behind my counter . . .' So I was in . . .
>
> Everybody loves the paua shell ball that you gave me, especially grandchildren . . . The family is really large now – it's rather like getting compound interest on a fortune . . .
>
> One of my co-grandmothers, the distinguished & lovable Dorothy Hodgkin, is going to a chrystallographers' conference in China. She lives in a wheelchair (rheumatoid arthritis). Her doctor said, 'You must not go. I can't guarantee that you will ever return.' Dossie said, 'I don't see the point of living if you can't even go to China when you feel like it.'

In June 1992 I spent a magical week with Winnie while I worked my way through relevant Davin papers. She was eighty-three, fragile, and needed time to recover from mounting or descending the stairs. But her spirit and her mind beamed as brightly as ever through her eyes and her animated face, and she was still brimful of mischief and fun. We made a nostalgic expedition to the Gardener's Arms with Anthony Stones, treated ourselves to lunches of salmon pieces, and ate strawberries while we watched the Wimbledon tennis on television.

Two years later she too was gone; and in the same week as Eric McCormick and Dan's sister Mollie and brother Martin. Again, that astonishment that what has character – and such character – can simply cease. The sense of loss became palpable for me in 1997 when, for the first time, I was back in England with no reason to visit Oxford. The thought of strangers in occupation at 103 Southmoor Road bordered on blasphemy. Naturally, one is grateful for the fruits of friendship and the memories one stores up. But the passage of those friends and the ending of relationships by death is the most difficult and the most perplexing aspect of living.

16.

Words at Robin Morrison's Funeral

1993

I have been to funerals, to what one could only describe as funereal funerals, at which speakers have taken the line that the less you expect from life, the less disappointed you'll be by its outcomes; that if you are a pessimist, your only surprises will be pleasant ones.

According to this school of thought, we're all born under sentence of death; life itself is a sexually transmitted terminal disease. According to *this* view, what Robin Morrison experienced was no more than a forty-eight-year reprieve.

I have been present, as I say, when things of this sort have been said. And I have to also say that they could not be less appropriate to an occasion such as this. Because nobody I know lived further removed from the shadow of mortality than Robin. His relationships, his conversations, his photography, were life-filled and life-enhancing, and redolent of warmth and humour. He helped us see the things we needed to see – things that made us knowing and tolerant and affectionate about our country; and he helped us see a great distance.

Even in the past eight months Robin declined the role of dying man. This was not blindness to what disease was doing to his body. It was a conscious choice about what aspects of life mattered; it was a reflection of the fact that, to the last, his spirit was undiminished and undefeated. His own verdict, reached and reiterated resolutely, was that 'you're not dead until you're dead'; and that if the quantity or length of lifespan was in question, then what mattered far more was its quality.

Having made that decision he faced what he faced with courage and grace. And in doing so he gave *us* the courage to face it. I felt frequently, during the months just past, that Robin was helping us, rather than vice versa. But that, while true, is also an overstatement. Because he was deeply conscious how much *he* was sustained and nourished by the network of family, friends and professional associations; and especially by family – by Dinah, Jake and Keir, Dorothy and Ashley, Dick and Julia.

I want, if I may, to speak personally for a few minutes. Like many others, I first encountered Robin through his work, in the pages of the *Listener*, where his astonishingly revealing photographs began to appear in the 1970s.

I remember especially one of Frank Sargeson, which did what no other portrait of the writer had done up to that time. I'm talking about the one of Frank sitting on his small verandah stroking his cat. It captured Sargeson's seriousness, and his extraordinary angularity. It showed, prominently but naturally, his writer's and gardener's hands. Close to those hands lay a green pepper, for which – among his friends – Frank was as famous as he was for his stories. And, even though he was dressed in what passed for his best clothes, it revealed that the writer's trousers were secured by a necktie. In addition to doing all these things, the photograph was beautifully composed, framing Frank in the leaves of his grapevine, through which the dappled light of summer was seen, but distanced.

Last year I found and read Frank's letter to the then *Listener* editor, Ian Cross, about that photo session. 'Morrison's a good lad,' Sargeson wrote. 'He knows what he's doing. There was no mucking about. And I enjoyed the time with him. Send him around again some time.' Robin's comment about the session was that Frank had been a ham, changing posture and expression for the camera with the ease and confidence of a professional model. (I must say here that, of all the fellow residents of the North Shore with whom I had linked and compared Sargeson, a connection with Rachel Hunter was one that hadn't previously occurred to me.)

The point is, of course, that it was Robin's easy presence and conversation that transformed Frank, temporarily, into that ham. Sargeson was not naturally a poser, though there was in him an element of poseur. There is a mountain of photographs that show him looking awkward or cross to testify that the success of that session was to the credit of the photographer rather than the subject.

Much later, working in collaboration with Robin, I saw the extent to which such successes were the product of highly refined instincts and skills. Robin had an extraordinary facility for putting people at their ease, and he did this largely by talking to them as he photographed. He also had a genius for snapping the shutter at the absolutely decisive moment when people, buildings and landscapes – and sometimes animals as well – arranged themselves into the composition that he had seen: or, more accurately, perhaps, foreseen.

I recall his photographing the Solomon brothers at Manukau in the Chathams, standing around the statue of their grandfather, the so-called last Moriori. The boys, the Beagle Boys, as they're known locally, were feeling a bit uncomfortable and didn't seem to know what to do with their hands. Robin kept talking to them and waiting. Suddenly, as Robin lifted the camera to his eye, they all three clasped their hands to the front, in unconscious imitation of the statue. The shutter clicked, and what Robin had was four Tommy Solomons, one of which happened to be in ferro-cement. The second after the picture was taken they were shuffling about again.

In addition to the technical mastery of his craft and the honing of his instincts, one of the things that made Robin such a fine photographer was his interest in the individuality and the variety of humanity. Nothing human was alien to him, in the words of the old Latin tag, and the more odd people were, the more they lived on the margins of society, the more they fascinated him. This did not lead him into the Diane Arbus territory of freak shows; nor did he ever photograph people in a manner that caricatured them or would have brought them embarrassment. But it did result in a large number of pictures of what could be called eccentrics, individuals whose very nonconformity was a comment on mainstream life and culture.

Sometimes his seeking out of such people led to incongruous results. He was keen to photograph the only woman professional fisherman on the Chathams, because she stood out as such a silhouette against the strongly male culture that prevails there. When he found her and did so, as she was rowing out to her boat, she shrieked with dismay and accelerated away from us. Because the last time she had seen Robin was also through the lens of a camera, when he had been drawn to her for similar qualities in another setting. She turned out to be Julia, the moon woman, whom he had photographed at the Fox River commune in 1979 for *The South Island of New Zealand from the Road.*

Inevitably, in my mind, professional recollections merge with personal ones. Robin was a marvellous person to work with, because he was the best of travelling companions. And he was the best of travelling companions because he derived so much joy from the shared rituals of friendship: from conversation, from good humour, from courtesy, from the preparation and enjoyment of good food and wine, from expeditions to interesting places, from the drink in the evening after a day's work; and from the quiet, companionable silences that exist between words and conversations.

All these things we shall miss; just as we shall miss the puckish sense of humour that infused so many of his photographs. Who, having seen it, can forget the picture of Norm Smith and his pet sheep Pebbles; and who, also having seen it, hasn't wondered which was Pebbles and which was Norm.

In this context, I must report that it was Robin who pointed out to me in Christchurch the advertising hording with the sinister message: 'Tellus – the last vaccum cleaner you'll need'; and underneath, in smaller print, the warning: 'Five year guarantee'. What, Robin asked, did vacuum cleaners know that we didn't?

We were also mutually delighted to discover that, at different times, we'd stayed in the same Dunedin hotel which had a notice on the vanity unit warning sternly: 'Guests are forbidden to hold praties in their rooms.' As New Zealanders of Irish extraction, we nursed an ancestral right to hold potatoes wherever we damn well liked. But it turned out that the 'a' and the 'r' had been transposed, and that what was prohibited was parties.

Mention of Ireland brings me to my final point. Next to New Zealand, which was in his bones, the country Robin most identified with was Ireland. He was proud of his Irish ancestry through his father. He sought and found Morrison relatives in Sligo. He took some of his best photographs there. He loved the work of James Joyce and William Butler Yeats. He was delighted to discover that his birthday, June 16, was Bloomsday – in *Ulysses* and in Dublin. I think it would not displease him to know that this commemoration of his life and work was taking place on that most extravagant of Irish festival days, the feast of St Patrick; and that the issue of the *Sunday Star* which reported his passing had a St Patrick's Day with the marvellous Irishism: 'abstinence is all very well, provided it's practised in moderation.'

The last time Robin stayed with me, towards the end of last year, we sat up late one night and talked about Ireland, and then read some of our favourite passages of Yeats to each other. One was the poem 'In Memory of Major Robert Gregory', of which I would like to quote three short stanzas. I trust that those of you who know their Yeats will forgive me for the alteration of just one line:

Now that we're almost settled in our house
I'll name the friends that cannot sup with us
Beside a fire of turf in th' ancient tower,
And having talked to some late hour
Climb up the narrow winding stair to bed:
Discoverers of forgotten truth
Or mere companions of my youth,
All, all are in my thoughts tonight being dead.

. . .

They were my close companions many a year,
A portion of my mind and life, as it were,
And now their breathless faces seem to look
Out of some fine picture book;
I am accustomed to their lack of breath,
But not that my dear old friend,
Our Sidney and our perfect man,
Could share in that discourtesy of death.

. . .

Some burn damp faggots, others may consume
The entire combustible world in one small room
As though dried straw, and if we turn about
The bare chimney is gone black out
Because the work had finished in that flare.
Artist, chronicler, visionary he,
As 'twere all life's epitome.
What made us dream that he could comb grey hair?

17.

The Kuia's Dying Day

1973

From the road I could see old Pare in black and the two small girls in bright skirts. They moved high on a King Country hillside littered with decaying logs and stumps, visible only as specks of colour against the bleak complexion of the landscape. They were facing the slope, bending over, straightening, walking a little and bending over again. They couldn't see me.

I left the car next to a tangle of pig fern and began to climb towards them. The rain had just stopped. Wet grass and stands of blackberry clung to my ankles as I moved. The cloud was still low and blurred the outline of the higher ridges. It was a desolate place – a rough, tiered surface and a forest cut down decades ago, left to rot. There was no sign of stock.

As I climbed, I remembered. It was two years since I had been to Honikiwi. Two years since I had paid the last of my visits to Pare and her mother, Nannie Taua, friend of King Tawhiao and the last of his protegees in the King Country.

Then, as on previous occasions, her mind was elsewhere when I arrived. She was hunched on the steps of her whare smoking a pipe, looking towards the ground and into a great distance. It took time to recall her from that other world which she longed to join; a world peopled with her tupuna and her contemporaries; with Tawhiao and Mahuta.

We called to her, Pare and I. After a time she looked up without recognition. Her face was solemn. Then her slow smile began at the mouth and spread to the cheeks and eyes. She remembered. 'Aie, tena koe, Michael, tena koe.' I clasped the bony hand and we hongied twice.

She was still arrestingly beautiful, even as she entered the last year of her life: the long, chiselled face; the rich brown skin whose wrinkles seemed as natural as grain patterns on varnished wood; the almond eyes that made her look more Asian than Polynesian; and the springy white hair plaited into pigtails. Her moko – emblem of her commitment to Maoritanga – was cut deep into her chin.

'E Nana. Michael's gong to Wellington. To Poneke,' Pare told her. 'He's come to say goodbye.'

Yes. I knew it would be goodbye. Not e noho ra, the farewell from one who is leaving to one who stays behind. This time I would say haere ra, goodbye to one who is going away. Although I was the one moving, I knew the old lady would not be waiting for me when I came back.

Nannie looked at me hard, trying to understand. 'To Poneke, ne? Aue, aue.' She began to cry and reached for my hand again. She held it tight in both of hers, as if unwilling to let me go. I felt the fragile life in her pressure and squeezed back, to try to give her some of my strength.

She began a waiata in a voice that quivered but kept the tune. I felt the hands tremble as she sang.

Kaore hoki koia te mamae
Te mutu noa
Ite wiki tahi
He tatau rangi.

The pain within me, longing for this loved one of mine, will never cease, said the song. Here I will dream of you, speak to you, embrace you, and then wake to find nothing but the rustling and whispering of the breeze. The ties that bind us now are torn suddenly.

Nannie's old whare, behind Pare's house, stood over a dirt floor. The wooden walls were unpainted and covered inside with pages from fashion magazines and the *Auckland Weekly*, some of them dating back fifty or sixty years. The chimney was corrugated iron. Two black kettles sat on iron bars in the fireplace and there was always a smoked eel hanging from a wire above. That's what I remember more than anything else about Nannie Taua's house – the smell of eels and ashes.

Pare was worried about the old woman sleeping out there on the ground by herself. 'She doesn't wake up till late in the morning. Sometimes I have to bend down and touch her face to make sure she's still warm.'

But Nannie wouldn't come inside the house with the rest of the family. And efforts to raise her standard of living had been wasted. 'We put a bed in there,' Pare explained. 'And she just moved her mat and blankets closer to the fire. Then we gave her an armchair but she had none of that either. She goes on squatting on the floor.' Habits of more than a century were not to be changed.

Nannie Taua was born in Honikiwi and raised her family there: eleven children of whom only four grew to adulthood. But she had travelled too. She went with Tawhiao to Hikurangi and Whatiwhatihoe – vast nineteenth-century settlements of which there is now no trace. She was in Kawhia when Tarawera erupted in 1886 and she thought it was gunfire, and in 1894 she walked nearly forty miles from Kawhia to Parawera for Tawhiao's tangi.

She talked about it once. It was the last long tangi in Waikato. The bound body lay in state at Parawera for three weeks. Mourners gathered in thousands. Nannie Taua, stripped to the waist and wreathed in koromiko leaves, called out her grief to them from beside the tupapaku.

Then she kept the old king company on his final journey through Waikato to Taupiri Mountain. The slow procession covered the distance in just under a week. At Taupiri they were greeted by thousands of additional mourners – the men and women of upper Waikato and visiting tribes. As the two groups met a band played a funeral march, rifles fired salutes and dynamite exploded on the mountain from the graveside. 'There will never be another like Tawhiao,' said Nannie Taua.

Nor will there be another like Nannie Taua. She had seen all these things. And yet she passed away without attention or tribute from the world, within sight of her birthplace and her parents' graves. Only a handful of family and friends mourned her at her own tangi.

A year later I was back, climbing the hill slowly, a lone mourner without the support of friend or whanau; as far as I knew, the only person from Poneke to lament the passing of Nannie Taua; perhaps the only one there who had heard of her.

When I was ten yards from Pare and the grandchildren I could see what they were doing. Still stooped with their backs to me, they were gathering huhu grubs from the crumbling logs. Even a wasted forest long dead was able to sustain life in a small way. The girls were putting the larvae into plastic bags filled with sawdust. Still they hadn't seen me.

I called out to Pare and waited. She stood up and turned around, staring at me. She was old herself now, in her mid-seventies. She looked like her mother but was more solid. And she had fewer wrinkles and no tattoo. The children, no taller than her knees, were clutching at her long black skirt, alarmed.

Then she recognised me and began to karanga – a cry of welcome that was at first strong and clear but became constricted as grief rose in her throat. I moved towards her slowly. And stopped, head bowed, as her sorrow ran over and she began to tangi, humming and dabbing her eyes with a white handkerchief.

When I went to her I took her hand and pressed noses for a long time in that most intimate of greetings, absorbing her grief and communicating mine to her. She began the high hum again away down in her throat and the tears came freely. Then she held me with both arms and leaned on me and said 'Michael, Michael,' over and over.

Later, we sat down on a flat stump. She held one of my arms and told me about Nannie Taua's tangi; about the tents, the mats, the food, the visitors and the speeches; and about the picture.

'You know that photo you gave me. The big one of Nannie with the pipe in her mouth. Well we put it behind the coffin in the whare mate, above her head. Do you know it misted over after the first manuhiri came. All except the nose. You could still see that. The young ones couldn't understand it and rubbed it clean. But it kept going misty. I knew what it was. I'd seen it happen when I was a girl. The old kuia was crying with us and her nose was pressing against the glass, hongi-ing with the people.'

As Pare was talking, the ceiling of cloud had lifted higher and uncovered to the top of the ribbed ranges. 'Look,' she said suddenly. 'The mountain's smiling.' I was jolted into a present that was an echo of the past: her mother had said exactly the same thing to me once before when the weather was clearing after a downpour.

I looked to the east and saw sunshine spreading down the shoulders of Pirongia from the summit to the foothills. As it came towards us, it heightened the blue of the bushed ridges and the green of the grassed slopes and pockets of second growth in the gullies. Even the grey logs about us whitened and became sharper as monotone gave way to light and shade.

We sat there – kuia, mokopuna and visitor; all touching. We warmed ourselves under the clearing sky and watched colour return to the land. Brighter now, it seemed unchanged since my last visit.

18.

Maori and Pakeha: Which People and Culture Has Primacy?

A paper presented at the Auckland Writers & Readers Festival, 2003

I'd like to begin by taking you back to that apocalyptic year all readers of George Orwell dreaded, 1984, when a much admired documentary by expatriate New Zealand journalist Michael Dean was shown on Television One. The thrust of the programme's message was that New Zealand Maori had been colonised by Europeans in the nineteenth century, and that some Maori resented the fact that this had occurred. No surprises there, you might think.

What *was* surprising, at least to those of us who know a bit of New Zealand history, was the nature of the evidence that Michael Dean selected to substantiate his thesis. You may remember that he gave us a lingering shot of the lone pine then growing on the summit of One Tree Hill. And he said that nothing better symbolised Maori grievances than this highly visible Auckland icon. The pine, he said, had been put there to replace a New Zealand totara, which had been chopped down. It was an *English* pine, he went on, signifying the subjection of Maori culture to that of the British invaders. To make this desecration worse, alongside the pine was a memorial to the Maori race, as if they were now an extinct phenomenon. The combination of these two features was an extreme provocation to Maori who lived within sight of the hill, he said.

Well, this presentation was a marvellous example of the kind of *misuse* of history that provokes in historians premature dementia. Dean's overall argument, about the British colonisation of New Zealand and about the fact that some Maori deeply resented that this had occurred, was, of course, valid. But the illustrative example he chose was almost wholly wrong.

There is traditional evidence from both Tainui and Ngati Whatua that a totara stood on the summit of One Tree Hill in the seventeenth and eighteenth centuries AD. By the time the Auckland isthmus was colonised by Europeans in the nineteenth century, the totara was gone and a pohutukawa stood in its place. That tree was cut down for firewood in 1852. In its place, John Logan Campbell planted another tree: a pohutukawa. He surrounded it with a ring of pines to protect it from the wind. *Californian* pines, *Pinus radiata*, not English ones. In the event, because of the exposed nature of the site, the pohutukawa and all but one of the pines died, leaving the summit of One Tree Hill with its second lone tree, a Californian pine. Far from being an attempt to erase a Maori emblem, the whole exercise had been designed – unsuccessfully as it turned out – to replace and renew that emblem.

As to the monument, Campbell's intention had been to honour tangata whenua. Like almost all Maori and Pakeha in the nineteenth century, he believed that the declining Maori population statistics indicated that Maori, as a people and as a culture, would soon disappear. Some Pakeha welcomed that outcome; others were indifferent; Campbell, however, mourned the prospect and wanted to salute Maori for the great people he believed they had been. And his successful determination to preserve the earthworks intact on Maungakiekie was part of his respectful salute to tangata whenua.

Can anyone who knows these facts characterise John Logan Campbell as a heartless and racist agent of colonisation who wanted to obliterate Maori culture? Michael Dean did, but then he hadn't done his homework. Mike Smith apparently believed the Dean slur too. Had he done *his* homework? Was he aware that surviving tangata whenua on the Auckland isthmus, Tainui and Ngati Whatua ki Tamaki Makaurau, saw nothing offensive about the lone pine or the obelisk? I don't know.

What this whole episode revealed, I think, is that history is more complex than the black-and-white, heroes-and-villains cartoon version beloved of journalists and activists. More complex, but infinitely more interesting as a consequence.

I have to say I felt a strong sense of déjà vu when I read about Joris de Bres's speech given last December on the first United Nations Day of Cultural Heritage. Can I remind you of what he alleged – or, rather, the part of what he alleged that attracted controversy.

'It is timely to recall,' he said, 'why UNESCO and the United Nations decided to focus this year on cultural heritage. It was in response to the cultural vandalism that led to the destruction of the Bamiyan Buddhas by the Taliban regime in Afghanistan. This was an appalling example of people of one culture wielding their power to destroy a site that was special to people of another. The world was outraged.

'But while we rightfully shake our heads in incomprehension and condemnation, the destruction of the Buddhas also challenges us to think of our own country and to examine our own record.'

My first reaction to hearing this was very similar to my reaction to the Michael Dean programme: the overall thesis may have been right – namely, that in the nineteenth century, Maori culture had not been accorded the respect from the colonising power that, by today's standards, we think it ought to have been. But what a way to dramatise this point.

Taken literally, as a commentary on lack of respect for material culture, namely the Buddha figures, de Bres's statement was one hundred per cent wrong, on several grounds.

First, destruction of pa sites aside, the only people who have deliberately destroyed or damaged cultural monuments in New Zealand in my lifetime have been Maori, anti-Semites daubing Jewish graves and a few deranged arsonists. The Maori examples I'm referring to are the statues of Sir George Grey in Albert Park and John Balance in Moutoa Gardens, both of which were beheaded; Te Miringa Te Kakara meeting house in the King Country, Rangiatea Church at Otaki and Awhitu House at Taumutu, all of which were burnt down by Maori; and the instance I've spoken about already, the tree on One Tree Hill.

Second, the only reason so many delicate examples of pre-European material culture have survived, particularly the wooden artefacts, is because of the efforts of European collectors, museums and art galleries to preserve them. Maori on the whole did not. For several reasons: one is that items regarded as tools or weapons were quickly discarded once European technology became available in the late eighteenth and early nineteenth centuries. A person offered a tomahawk would willingly trade it for a carved wooden or bone wahaika, or simply discard the wahaika. Another is that items that came into the category of heirlooms – hei tiki or patu pounamu, perhaps – would sometimes be passed down through generations; but they might just as likely be buried with a current owner as a mark of respect for both the owner and the taonga. It was left to interested European to preserve items which represented the art and craft skills of pre-contact Maori, many of which would be seen by Maori as taonga only after the passage of a lengthy period of time. Something like ninety-five per cent of the items in the *Te Maori* exhibition, which showcased pre-contact Maori culture to the world, had been preserved and protected by Pakeha individuals or institutions – a fact scarcely analogous to the example of the Taliban's attitude to the Bamiyan Buddhas.

For these reasons, and for the fact that our (then) allies had just been to war with the Taliban in the wake of September 11, I felt de Bres's comparisons of New Zealand Pakeha behaviour with that of Islamic fundamentalists was singularly inappropriate. And I have to say I also thought they were inappropriate for someone in a role that was formerly known as Race Relations *Conciliator* – but that's a separate issue.

When I came to read Joris de Bres's *full* speech, of course, it was to find that the examples he gave of Pakeha destructiveness were not, as in the case of the Taliban, destruction of Maori *material* culture; but instead a failure to respect the *non*-material culture – values, concepts, view of the world, waahi tapu. That of course is a valid argument to make, though the historian in me would add some qualifications.

One is that in making the judgements de Bres does about European attitudes to Maori culture in the nineteenth century and later, he is applying the knowledge and the insights and the concepts of the twenty-first century to a time when *that* intellectual landscape was absent. It rather reminds me of the lecturer I once heard criticising the behaviour of Native Minister John Bryce in 1881 as lacking in the kinds of insights shown by Mahatma Gandhi and Martin Luther King.

I would also caution that rather than speak in terms of 'Maori good' and 'Pakeha bad', one should recognise that colonisation is a process that is capable of dehumanising both coloniser and colonised. What was it Lord Acton had to say about the effect of the exercise of power?

To see the truth of this, we don't have to examine just *Pakeha* behaviour. We only have to look at the one example we have of *Maori* in the role of colonisers. In the nineteenth century there were three Maori proposals that we know of to go offshore and relocate tribes in other parts of the Pacific: one was capture Norfolk Island, another to attack Western Samoa, and a third to move to the Chatham Islands. The Chathams venture was the only one of these that was actioned, when Ngati Tama and Ngati Mutunga hijacked a European ship in Wellington Harbour in 1835 and forced the captain to transport 900 men, women and children to Chatham Island, the largest in the group: to live there and to colonise the indigenous Moriori.

What did they do when they got there? Did they respect the mana and mana whenua of the tangata whenua? Did they offer them a partnership in which the islands could be developed as the joint homes of both peoples? Did they respect the sacred places and the economic resources of Moriori people? Did they, in other words, behave the way Maori expected Europeans to behave towards them in the nineteenth century?

In a word, no. After being welcomed by Moriori, who also nursed their sick, Ngati Tama and Ngati Mutunga attacked their hosts, who had outlawed warfare. They ritually killed some ten per cent of an unresisting population, a ritual that included staking out women and children along the beachfront at Waitangi and leaving them there to die over several days in great pain. They enslaved the surviving population. They forbade wives to cohabit with husbands and parents with children. They forbade the speaking of the Moriori language. They forced Moriori to desecrate their sacred sites by urinating and defecating on them. The combined effect of all these measures was that the Moriori population plummeted from 1600 to half a dozen by the end of the nineteenth century. Stella Cotter, a descendant of one of the survivors, said to me, 'If only *we'd* had a Treaty of Waitangi. If only *we'd* been colonised by the English.' Oddly enough, once the Chathams *did* come into the orbit of the New Zealand Government and civil service in 1842, it took a further sixteen years before slavery was abolished on the islands and Moriori were given what is described in article three of the Treaty of Waitangi as 'the royal protection and . . . the Rights and Privileges of British Subjects' – all of which Maori had had since 1840.

The final disaster for Moriori was that when the Chathams at last had court sittings, the Native Land Court in 1870, Maori were awarded more than ninety-seven per cent of the islands' land by right of conquest. So the Moriori's 500 years of uninterrupted occupation meant nothing in the face of what had happened there five years before the signing of the Treaty of Waitangi.

Now I go over all that not with a view to being anti-Maori – but as an antidote to the view some have that Maori were the noble victims of colonial rapacity, and that they behaved at all times equitably and honourably in their dealings with others. They behaved, in fact, as one would expect, according to the dictates of tikanga Maori; and tikanga Maori dictated that you most respected people who were as capable of inflicting destruction on you as you were on them. It's sad but telling, I think, that the nineteenth-century Maori expression for Moriori was Paraiwhara – Blackfellas.

By contrast, one has to say that while there were cultural, political and social deficits, particularly in the ways that land was wrested from Maori once Pakeha settlers were in control, and in the impact of viral and bacteriological diseases, the formal European colonisation of New Zealand was founded on attempts to be fair; and that colonisation delivered much of benefit to Maori. Far from being the passive victims of the 'fatal impact' scenario, Maori from the time of initial contact with Europeans were competitive, energetic and enterprising, and showed a genius for taking what was of value from the ideas and technologies of the Western world and turning those things to their advantage.

After the kinds of history to which we have been subjected now for three decades, that which sought to document and emphasise the negative effects of colonisation on Maori, I hope we will soon see a swing of the pendulum that explores the strategies by which Maori coped with European colonisation and coped so well – particularly in contrast with the examples of some other indigenous people in, say, North and South America and Australia.

Coped *so* well, in fact, that we still have, more than one hundred and sixty years after formal colonisation began, two broad cultural streams in New Zealand – Maori and Pakeha – that can be distinguished from one another, and that still in so many respects display different priorities and different values. And the kinds of issues I have been talking about, including the furore surrounding Joris de Bres's Taliban statement, indicate that we have yet to negotiate a social contract with which both peoples are comfortable.

In case that all sounds too polemical – and those arguments *are* more polemical than I intend them to be – let me approach the topic again from another direction.

Occasionally, just occasionally, historians have epiphanic experiences in which the past seems very close to the present. John Beaglehole spoke of just such an experience he had in 1939, when he walked part of the Coromandel coast from Kennedy Bay to Whitianga, then on to Cooks Beach, where James Cook and his astronomer had observed the transit of the planet Mercury across the face of the sun in November 1769.

The next morning was absolutely crystalline, Beaglehole wrote,

> the sea and the sand as pure as the air and the early sun; and I walked along the beach by the side of the sea, round that magnificent curve, up to the edge of what James Cook called Oyster River. On the other side of the stream two or three Maori figures appeared and looked

> at me: otherwise the whole bay, from sea to the hills, was empty and silent. And yet I felt something. It was nothing to do with a half-stirring breeze, or the gradually warming sun, though it *was* a sort of faint tingling of the mind.
>
> It was an experience I have had only twice at other times: once crossing Botany Bay, also on a clear calm morning, the other on a blazing hot day on a beach below casuarina trees on Tahiti. I don't want to use that old expression 'the trembling of a veil', but it was like that. And on the other side, just beyond my vision, was a ship, and a boat rowing towards the shore; and somewhere or other, just floating beyond the reach of my ear, was the sound of words. I almost, before I turned back, caught sight of the *Endeavour*, I almost heard the words of eighteenth-century sailors . . .

I hope I don't strain your credulity, or entirely demolish my own authority, if I tell you that I too, like most historians, have had similar experiences. One also involved James Cook. On the kind of morning John Beaglehole describes, on the stretch of Coromandel coastline where *we* live, we had a telephone call from a neighbour. 'Go out to your balcony and look out to sea,' he said. We did. What we saw was entirely unexpected. The *Endeavour* replica was sailing past, en route from Tauranga to Auckland. As we looked down the sightline from our balcony, down the estuary, across the sandspit and out to sea where the *Endeavour* glided with billowed sails, there was nothing visible of the twentieth century. Even more extraordinary, the entire view was framed, left and right, by the branches of ancient pohutukawa with flax-like epiphytes, which may well have been there over two hundred years ago. One had a sense of time collapsing, of looking down a corridor into the eighteenth century and seeing exactly what Maori eyes had seen from that coast 230 years before. And what one saw was a maritime artefact of live charisma and great beauty.

Another experience of this kind, and the one that is relevant to today's reflections, occurred in an office of the University of Auckland's new arts building, between Symonds and Wynyard Streets. I was cloistered there one weekend afternoon, writing a narrative that became a history of Catholics in New Zealand. As I was struggling to read from a French journal that described the visit to Doubtless Bay of Jean de Surville and his crew in 1769, I was disturbed by a noise behind me, out in Wynyard Street. I couldn't determine the meaning of that noise – it was generated by a congregation of male voices and muffled by two brick walls; but it was obtrusive enough to make concentration difficult.

I made a deliberate effort to focus my attention back on the French text. This is what I read, written by Jean Pottier de l'Horme, an officer of the French India Company on board de Surville's vessel. He was describing his fellow countrymen making their first landing in Doubtless Bay.

> All [the] people were scattered here and there on the hills and the shore, and were no doubt doing honour to the new arrival[s] by waving . . . branches of grass . . . to one side, as though to create a breeze . . . [It] started right from when they first saw the boat, and went on until the captain set foot on land.

I went on to read l'Horme's opinion that, while these people, the Ngati Kuri of Karikari Peninsula, appeared to be 'savages', and of 'limited intelligence', he felt sure that if they were exposed to the light of true religion and the gifts of European civilisation, they would drop such barbarous habits as waving greenery at strangers as they came ashore.

At this point the noise outside reached a pitch of obtrusiveness so I went to the windows at the rear of the building to see what was causing it. The source was the University of Auckland Maori Club spread out along much of the length of Wynyard Street, practising for a powhiri that was to take place later that day. And in their hands they held small branches with green leaves, which they waved as they chanted, '*as though to make a breeze*', in Pottier de l'Horme's words.

So there I was and there were they. At the very moment of reading the opinion of an informed eighteenth-century European that Maori, if colonised, would drop such barbaric habits as powhiri – at that very moment I was hearing and witnessing an educated group of Maori of the kind envisaged by Pottier de l'Horme, and they were delivering a powhiri in essentially the same manner as their predecessors had done 228 years earlier at Doubtless Bay.

It was a moment I recalled not long afterwards when I read a marvellous passage by the American historian Arthur Schlesinger junior. It goes like this:

'History haunts even generations who refuse to [acknowledge it]. Rhythms, patterns, continuities, drift out of time long forgotten to mould the present and to colour the shape of things to come.' This observation is as profoundly true of New Zealand in the twenty-first century AD as it is of anywhere else in the world where humankind has managed to survive in home places for lengthy periods of time. As is so often the case in history, elements of *continuity* are as noticeable and as interesting as elements of change.

And there are others. The strong degree of tribal competitiveness that delayed the distribution of fishing quota by the Waitangi Fisheries Commission; the appetite for martial behaviour that animates urban Maori gangs and makes the New Zealand Army a popular Maori career choice; the admiration of people who are cheeky and cunning in the mould of Maui-tikitiki-a-Taranga; the easy resort to song and story when there are messages of a communal kind to be transmitted; the continuing weight of unwritten tikanga or tradition; the I-am-we ethos of tribal culture in which the corporate self is more important than individual identity. All these elements are part of the 'rhythms, patterns and continuities' that drift out of time past to leave an imprint on the Maori present.

And what is true of Maori culture is also true of that of *Pakeha* New Zealanders. A myriad of echoes of old New Zealand still resonate within the *contemporary* culture. The 'man alone' ideal, the hunting/shooting/fishing ethic, and that of the solitary bachelor, survive in New Zealand from the frontier days, when, partly because of the shortage of women, many men lived that way; the bach culture based on a strong desire to live simply on the margin between land and sea, or between tamed and untamed places; the home-maintenance tradition that sets men to work on houses, boats and gardens; the fiercely egalitarian instinct which prefers to see resources spread widely and equitably throughout the community and not, as elsewhere, in massive disproportion between the very rich and the very poor; the reactions of dissenting individuals or groups in the face of authority; the largely informal social attitudes. All these phenomena have a history which can be linked back to the attitudes and values formed in the nation's years of gestation in the nineteenth century.

Both collections of habits, values and attitudes have sufficient force to be called traditions. And both give New Zealand an ongoing bicultural character over and above the forces which, in other contexts, make the country multicultural. Multiculturalism too is a reality, in the sense that Maori culture is tribal rather than nationally homogeneous; and Pakeha culture is made up of many strands, some of which – the Scottish, the Irish, the Jews, the Chinese – may wish to retain active links with their cultures of origin; and in the sense that the quality of being a Maori, a Pacific Island, a Gujarati or a Jewish New Zealander may differ markedly.

But the dominant realities of New Zealand life are still a mainstream Pakeha culture, in which almost every citizen has to participate in order to be educated, secure employment, play sport, and engage in most other forms of recreation; and a tangata whenua culture in which the language, rituals of encounter and ways of farewelling the dead are still markedly different from those of the Pakeha majority, and more visible and pervasive than those of other minority cultures. In addition Maori *is* the foundation human culture of the land, the first repository of its namings and its histories and its songs; and it *is* the culture of the people who have, for as long as they want it, a special relationship with the government of New Zealand via the Treaty of Waitangi – a relationship which other peoples and cultures, including the Pakeha majority, lack. Whether other cultures *need* or *want* or are *deserving* of such a relationship is another matter. The fact is that the Treaty of Waitangi is unmistakably still there after more than one hundred and sixty years; and its significance and relevance is ensured by a Maori insistence, accepted by the current Government, that the document mediates a *living* relationship between Maori and the Crown, and by a majority Pakeha view that this constitutes an appropriate stance for the country to take. Should either of those views change, then the significance and the potential power of the Treaty too would change; because they are dependent for their force on the consent of those two constituent peoples.

Having passed through an era, pre-1970s, in which the Treaty of Waitangi was *not* observed or honoured, however, and into one in which that deficit is being rectified, there is now a strong Pakeha aspiration for the values and imperatives of *their* culture too to be recognised and taken as seriously by the government and the country as a whole as tangata whenua culture. In part, this impulse comes from a growing conviction on the part of Pakeha that their culture, like that of Maori, is no longer the same as the cultures of origin from which it sprang – that is has become, in fact, a second indigenous culture by the same processes by which East Polynesian people developed Maori culture: transplanting imported concepts and values from one place to another, observing those things change over time in relationship to a new land and new circumstances, and eventually focusing attention away from the ancestral home and fully on the contemporary homeland.

That this increased valuing of their own heritage should lead Pakeha to become advocates for their culture is perhaps something of a surprise. The assumption most of us grew up with was that Pakeha culture was strong enough and pervasive enough to persist through and despite of any vicissitudes or challenges it might encounter. And perhaps it is. We imagined that the special measures undertaken as a Treaty obligation to protect and strengthen *Maori* language and culture were necessary because of their vulnerability; and that such measures would not in any way threaten the existence or the viability of Pakeha culture.

But then a series of decisions, none of them directly related, appeared to suggest that a former imbalance was being corrected by the creation of another imbalance. In 1999, the same month that the National Museum, Te Papa Tongarewa, refused to remove the Virgin in a Condom from display in a visiting exhibition of contemporary British art, which was giving strong offence to some Christians, the Waikato Museum of Arts and History withdrew a Dick Frizzell exhibition because moko on the face of a caricatured Four Square grocer offended Tainui kaumatua.

Three years later Transit New Zealand postponed work on State Highway One near Mercer on the grounds that local Tainui people believed such work would disturb a taniwha, at almost the same time the North Shore City Council announced that it would proceed with the widening of Esmonde Road in Takapuna, even though the widening process would carve twelve metres off the front of Frank Sargeson's section, including the legendary 'hole in the hedge' and the area of former garden in which his ashes have been interred.

Both sets of events arose from different decisions by different officials in different institutions. But the ones in favour of Maori interests all grew out of Treaty-based obligations in legislation or mission statement undertakings to consult with Maori interests and to observe the principles of the Treaty of Waitangi. In the case of roading issue, the relevant factor was the obligation to respect wahi tapu or sacred places.

Most Pakeha, I would submit, accept the need for that obligation. I certainly do. The problem they identify is that the country now has legislatively based procedures to protect the values and sensibilities of one culture and not the other. They do not want to see anything taken away from Maori in this context, just to see the measures of protection and respect extended from the one culture to embrace both cultures – I personally would like to see New Zealand English given the same protection and emphasis as New Zealand Maori. I want to see wahi tapu of significance to Pakeha, such as Frank Sargeson's grave, given as much protection as wahi tapu of significance to Maori; and I want the history and experience of Pakeha New Zealanders to be valued by the country as a whole, and by its institutions, as much as those of Maori.

I am asking, in other words, for what my colleague Michael Ignatieff has referred to in another context as a 'mutuality of respect'. And as another manifestation of that respect, I would also expect Maori to critique Pakeha culture and Pakeha heritage with same care and sensitivity as we Pakeha are asked, and agree, to extend to things Maori. Just as Pakeha are now decades away from the stance which viewed Maori culture as 'primitive', 'backward' or 'barbaric', so Pakeha ought not to be currently viewed by Maori as tauiwi, aliens, or representatives of a colonising power that merely stole material and cultural resources from Maori and gave nothing in return.

In fact the two cultures are still in a relationship of mutual exchange that began as early as 1769. Contemporary Maori culture is as strong as it is in its renascent form in part because of the ability of its adherents to select successfully from the range of concepts and technologies that the Western world – initially Europeans – had to offer, and to incorporate those things into their culture on the basis of Maori needs and concepts of usefulness. One early and spectacular example is the Maori use of photography to take the place of ancestral representations in carvings in meeting houses and elsewhere, and consequently strengthen the ability of the culture to remember and revere ancestors. The modern Maori concept of tino rangatiratanga, of what we would now recognise as *corporate* tribal authority, developed because the Westminster parliamentary system of one person-one vote could not coexist with the mid-nineteenth-century concept of *chiefly* authority, which was what Henry Williams had in mind when he designed the term for the text of the Treaty of Waitangi. This of course means that the tino rangatiratanga that the Treaty promised to protect is not the tino rangatiratanga that contemporary Maori seek to have delivered. But there is nothing out of the ordinary in that: cultures, *all* cultures that are alive, change over time, and their words change their meaning. The Maori culture of the twenty-first century is not Maori culture frozen at 1769, nor at 1840. Nor should it be. It changed and grew dynamically according to changing needs and circumstances prior to the eighteenth century. And it continues to do so.

Similarly Pakeha culture continues to borrow and to learn from Maori. That is one of the features that makes it different from its European cultures of origin. It borrows words and concepts (mana, tapu, whanau, taonga, turangawaewae, tai hoa); attitudes (the tradition of hospitality which, in the early nineteenth century, was so much more visible from the Maori side of the frontier than the Pakeha); ways of doing business (an increasing willingness to talk issues through to consensus in preference to dividing groups 'for' and 'against' a given motion); and rites of passage (a loosening up of formerly formal and highly structured funeral services).

There is, as yet, no sign of the cultures bringing an end to these exchanges; just as there is no sign that, despite the exchanges, the different characters and flavours of the cultures will dilute or disappear in the near future. Keith Holyoake's vision for the twenty-first century of a single race and culture of brown-skinned New Zealanders living the 'best of both heritages' is as far away now as it was when he made his prediction in the 1960s. The bicultural reality remains a given which all New Zealanders need to be informed about, and through which they will have to continue to negotiate – as national governments, as local governments, as community organisations and as individuals.

And *most* New Zealanders, I believe, whatever their cultural background, are good-hearted, commonsensical and tolerant. And those qualities are part of the national cultural capital that has in the past saved the country from the worst excesses of racism and ethnic conflict seen in other parts of the world; and it is a sound basis for optimism about the country's future.

Frank Sargeson always said there were two ways of communicating: nakedly direct or baroquely oblique. No prize for guessing which route *he* favoured. I too have chosen the long way round. And it brings me now, to the rhetorical question which lies in the background of this talk: which of the two indigenous New Zealand cultures has primacy?

Neither culture, in my view, has or deserves primacy in the sense of having a right to dominate or control the other. Maori and Pakeha in New Zealand are in a relationship in the nature of siblings: tuakana and teina, to use the Maori expressions for older and younger brothers or sisters. The tuakana culture does deserve respect for being here first, of being the longest occupiers of the land and the people who first gave that land names and history. That is an acknowledgement most Pakeha are prepared to make, I think, especially when that occupation has been lengthy and continuous on the part of a single kinship group – Tuhoe in the Urewera for example. The tuakana culture also has the right to expect the state to respect and protect those things promised protection in the Treaty of Waitangi, particularly cultural taonga such as Maori language.

The teina culture, Pakeha, deserves no special consideration on account of being the younger or the less experienced in its occupation of the country; and certainly not on the grounds of being a more advanced culture, as some of our European forebears rather witlessly believed. Outside the conditions arising specifically from the text of the Treaty, however, I see the two predominant cultures as deserving of equal consideration. They are still, as I have indicated, in a symbiotic relationship in which each has *enriched* the other to a far greater degree than either has injured or diminished the other; and one hopes that kind of relationship will persist.

They *both* deserve respect; and, specifically, *each deserves the respect of the other*. And it is on that repeated note, of mutuality of respect, that I shall finish, and I thank you for your attention.

Acknowledgements

'Being Pakeha' was first published in *Pakeha: The Quest for Identity in New Zealand*, edited by Michael King, Penguin, 1991; 'Contradictions' was first published in *One of the Boys?: Changing Views of Masculinity in New Zealand*, edited by Michael King, Heinemann, 1988; 'Back to Shul' was first published in *At the Edge of Memory: A Family Story*, by Michael King, Penguin, 2002; 'What I Believe' was first published in *What I Believe: The Personal Philosophies of Twenty-two New Zealanders, compiled* by Allan Thomson, GP Publications Ltd, 1993; 'Jerusalem 25 October 1972' was first published in *James K. Baxter 1926–1972: A Memorial Volume*, Alister Taylor Publishing, 1972; 'Tangata Whenua: Origins and Conclusions' was first published in *Landfall*, edited by Peter Smart, 121:March 1977; 'Approaching a Distant Peak: A Biographer Discovers Frank Sargeson' was first published in *An Affair of the Heart: A Celebration of Frank Sargeson's Centenary*, edited by Graeme Lay and Stephen Stratford, Cape Catley, 2003; 'Yet Being Someone Other' was first published in *New Zealand Listener*, 23 March 2002; 'A Life Touched by Angels and Shadows' was first published in *Sunday Star-Times*, 1 February 2004; 'Remembering Dan and Winnie Davin' was first published in *Intimate Stranger: Reminiscences of Dan Davin*, edited by Janet Wilson, Steele Roberts, 2000; 'The Kuia's Dying Day' was first published in *Te Maori*, 1973. All reproduced with kind permission, where appropriate. All other works are previously unpublished.

The King family would like to thank the helpful staff of the Alexander Turnbull Library and the National Library, and Geoff Walker and Jeremy Sherlock at Penguin.

Index